PANNING FOR THE GOLD OF WISDOM

By Alice Spohn Newton

GOLDEN QUILL PRESS
Publishers Since 1902
Manchester Center, Vermont

Golden Quill Press
Manchester Center, Vermont

Alice Spohn Newton, 1996, All rights reserved

Library of Congress Catalog Number 96-75067

I.S.B.N. 0-8233-0507-4

Printed in the United States of America

PANNING FOR THE GOLD OF WISDOM

OTHER BOOKS
BY ALICE SPOHN NEWTON

Paths Of Wondering
A Bowl Of Remembering
Then The Moon Began To Sing
Have A Cup Of Bygoners
My Song Of Many Loves
On The Wings Of Tomorrow
The Reminding Wind
The Nonconforming Professor
Christ Is A Close Companion
Whatever Happened To God's Very Good?
I Love Those Indians
God Having Fun
How To Make Earth Heaven
Live Knowing You Have Forever
The Chocolate Hill
The Sun Says When
A Tour Of The Blossoming Prairie
The Handle Of The Pan

CONTENTS

What Is God For? 1

The Chocolate Hill 4

I Love Those Indians 7

Have A Cup of Bygones 20

He Thinks Trees Think 26

The Reminding Wind 30

God Having Fun 34

The Nonconforming Professor 40

Paths of Wondering 50

A Tour of The Blossoming Prairie 53

Live Knowing You Have Forever 54

The Handle of The Pan 56

What Happened To God's Very Good? 59

On The Wings of Tomorrow 64

Christ As A Close Companion 67

My Song of Many Loves 70

How To Make Earth Heaven 73

A Bowl of Remembering 76

The Last Kink of Civilization 79

PREFACE

The trail of Time leading to the panning of gold is longer than recorded. Even longer, man has sought through the stones of general belief for wisdom, that which stands as undimmed as gold. We will never stop panning for enduring truths to be lain on the table of Time where those who partake are blessed.

For authors this is particularly true. Books have to be made on this panning precept. Publishers glean with utmost care, that a nugget of falsehood doesn't slip by.

So as much as an author loves to write (he wouldn't if he didn't) he must pan thoroughly his ideas and inspirations to work only with pure gold truth nuggets.

It is awe-inspiring that whatever talent one is born with, our Truth Planner is a part of the equipment. A sculptor's eyes and hands pan for the gold of something beautiful, faultless, inspiring; and he can't quit till his dream is fulfilled which is nothing short of perfection.

This is true also of an artist with his paints and empty canvas. The gleaning and inner vision go on until the portrait or scene is as perfect as he can make it.

The joy of this divine feeling for perfection is that no one is born without, the screening pan for what's best. No one should let the panning for the best rust from misuse.

The contents of the following pages are all of the author's eighteen published books *condensed into one volume,* panned till only the nuggets of lasting gold are left. She longs that the reader be blessed by such prudent panning.

—*Alice Spohn Newton*

CHAPTER 1

WHAT IS GOD FOR?
(From: The Sun Says When, Published by Marshall Jones Company, 1994)

Lorna Gerard stood by the spraying fountain in the railroad station park where she could gaze at the brilliant sunset. The bright run-together reds, yellows, and blues of the sky appeared as calm and compassionate as a very needed friend here at the end of the day.

Life seemed over.

How horribly impersonal and matter-of-fact divorce proceedings are! The pudgy, indifferent Judge must have been planning what he was going to order for lunch. He didn't even look at her. It was just another divorce case running into the noon hour to him. He might at least have asked if there were children, if her husband had abused her, just to have kept the divorce from being so ridiculously easy and of no importance.

Well, she was free…the fights and deep slashes of hate were over. But what now?

She was suddenly without purpose. The Judge in his calm, everyday way, had blotted out the past, leaving nothing but a future as blank as an artist's canvas when he didn't know what to paint. Somehow Lorna wished she could slowly fade from existence.

But, no. Surely somehow she could find a way, a new purpose to go on. Like going to Denver, no reason except it was a place.

Her eyes caught sight of a small boy coming directly to her.

"Lady, could you spare a dime?"

"What's the matter, dad out of a job?" she asked.

"Don't even know where he is."

"Oh. Then you're helping a deserted mother."

"Nope. Mom's dead. I'm on the road," he boasted…See that freight over there? As soon as it starts movin', I'm hoppin' it," he bragged.

"Heavens, son, isn't there any other way?" Lorna exploded, a small child hopping trains!

"Nope. It suits a fella like me. I ain't goin' to no orphans' home. Would you?"

"But your father?"

"Him and Mom de-vorced. Couldn't even find him when Mom died. Besides, it's swell hoppin' freights. You oughtta try it," he suggested in his friend-to-friend way.

Lorna handed him a dollar.

"Boy! Are you rich?"

"No. But you may need that before you get your next dime."

"Thank you! Whole gobs. Gee, that's swell," he grinned.

"Be careful," she called as he ran for the opened-door freight car.

"Awm good at it. Watch me!" He waved his arm as he ran toward the puff-starting train.

Suddenly the car jerked as he waved and out the boy tumbled.

"Oh, God!" Lorna screamed and scrambled across tracks to his body which had been hurled with force.

"Get an ambulance," someone said.

A man stepped forth and took the boy in his arms. "Is he your child?" he asked.

"Yes," she cried defiantly, feeling suddenly that he was and could be taken from her.

The ambulance rolled in quickly…then with its wailing siren announcing human distress, sped on.

"Concussion and broken arm," someone said. "Operate at once."

Lorna was awed to realize that now her whole existence seemed to rest upon the fate of the little freight-hopping boy.

If a grim-faced nurse came in and announced, ALL OVER, what then?

What would she do if he lived?

A nurse came. "Would you give me the child's name, please?"

"Is he going to live?"

"Likely. But what is the boy's name?"

"I don't know."

"You don't know?"

"But I'll take the responsibility of expenses," Lorna stated firmly.

"I was told he was your son. What is your name?"

"Lorna Gerard."

"Address?"

"I don't know—Guess I'll check in at the Jefferson Hotel."

"I wonder if you would come with me to the office," the nurse started forth. "A form must be filled out."

It came to her that she could claim him as her son. Of course. No reason in the world not to!

But then if he died…It would be too shattering. What more!

Deep down she knew her purposeless feeling came from her and Martin not having children. "I'm a mom by nature."

The nurse came again. "If you wish to see the boy, you may come with me."

After a long, long time he opened his eyes.

"Hi," Lorna said. "That freight you hopped gave a sudden jerk and off you flew, hitting the ground with a crash!"

He seemed to have heard her, even remembering their few moments together in which she made him so pleased with his dollar.

"Tell me, son. What is your name?" she asked.

"Jerry."

"Last name?"

"Stephens."

It was soon clear that adoptions were not easy, especially when one parent was dead and the other a deserter. A long wait was needed to advertise for the whereabouts of the father. His consent had to be given unless it became impossible for him to be located.

Jerry got well, came to live with her, even sold papers to "help out."

Had there ever been a more compatible Mom and son relationship?

Then one night he was late. The papers must not have sold too fast.

Never had he been so late. That hot dog, That Wild West Show. Something was wrong!

Finally he burst in but there was no smile. His lips were tense and he had a look of fear in his eyes. "My dad's outside. He said I had no right letting a stranger adopt me. He says I gotta go with him."

"Where did he come from?" she asked in shock, remembering the months trying to find him.

"He came up to buy a paper. I didn't recognize him but he knew me right off!"

The man stepped inside. He was tall, bulky, with sandy hair and a mustache. "How could you adopt without my consent?" he asked sharply.

"By serving public notice according to law. Jerry is legally mine…I have adoption papers to prove it."

"Huh!" the father glowered. Turning to Jerry, he said, "If you've got any man in you, you'll come with your own dad, now that he's finally found you!"

Jerry was terrified. He looked at Lorna. He couldn't speak.

Tenseness gripped them all.

"Which'll it be?" the man demanded.

Tears rolled down Jerry's cheeks. He cried, "Guess I oughtta go with pop."

There were things she was sure she could do to get the child back. But he had gone. He had gone!

The days dragged on until Lorna could stand it no longer. She must move to a different place…

It was an hour before her train would be leaving. Should she or shouldn't she go?

Nothing had answers. The sweetest bliss was now the bitterest!

Suddenly, someone nearby said, "That bum out there in that freight car, he's just a kid!"

Lorna looked up. "Jerry! Jerry!"

He saw her. "Mom!" He jumped. She caught him.

"You know what, Mom? You made me go to Sunday School and I prayed and God did it. God did it!"

"Yes, my precious son, that's what God's for. That's why we pray! Oh, God! Oh, God!"

It was all she could say.

CHAPTER 2

THE CHOCOLATE HILL
(Published by Marshall Jones Company, 1994)

A GLIMPSE OF THE GREAT DEPRESSION

In California there it was, a hill shaped like a chocolate drop, bare and seemingly useless for growing any vegetation.

Jale Albin sat on a stump at the top in the shade of Bucket, the old horse hitched to the harrow. How did the horse get up there? The horse strained hoof at a time on the path with its winding slant; needed, he could do it. After beans then squash, peas, cabbage, then the tomato plants Mom was so proud of, all money saved for shoe soling, etc.

Jale looked toward the old shack behind the pepper tree Mom had set out in front of which was Mom's clothesline decorated with shirts and dingy underwear. Jale's Old Man was wrestling with one of the tires on the dilapidated truck on a dug-out place at the bottom of the hill.

Maybe he'd tell the Old Man to take his hill and go to hell. If he got away from the hill he could get a job and have a place of his own. Marry Vivian and get somewhere!

He laid down on the soft ground and wished he could pull the sky down on top of him so everything would go away.

His and Roland's room tacked on to the shack was hardly big enough for their cot, let alone making room for Vivian.

Life was like an apple, firm and bright and tart. Good to eat. But if it stayed in the sack too long the apple grew brown inside, soft.

You bit into one and then threw it away…That was what life was like. The farther you were pushed back the bigger the rotten got. He knew. His Old Man and Old Lady had grown rotten in all the struggling. Cranky, bitter, without hope.

Yet, the Old Man in his cowboy hat must have been the hardest apple a fellow could bite into, setting out to conquer the whole West. But kids, rent, no job kept shoving him back till they didn't have a dime. The whole country broke.

They saw the Chocolate Hill and thought about planting things on top where nobody even thought he could climb.

"The hill's the thing that's done it," Jale said.

"So now that things are better…"

He sat up. Why didn't he marry and strike out on his own?

The Old Man with his wrench was hollering for him to get back to work.

"Go to hell!" he glowered, and he felt so good he started singing. "Casey Jones…"

Maybe after he married he would land a job picking oranges that he could eat now and then! How could he get where he wanted to go if he didn't get up and do it! This wasn't his place.

By the time the sun had dropped behind the hill Jale was combing beans from the edge of the hill, the job done!

The Old Lady was yelling, "Supper!" and the Old Man was sitting in his bashed-in chair re-reading an old newspaper.

The smell of cabbage was stifling.

After supper Jale changed into his green shirt and brown cotton trousers he was so proud of and said he was going.

"Where?" the Old Man yelled.

"To see my girl."

"What girl?"

"Any girl."

When he reached the highway he saw Foo coming in his antiquated black truck, so he waved. Foo stopped and waited wordlessly for him to get in.

In the outskirts of San Pedro, Foo stopped and let Jale out.

"See ya!" Jale said as he walked hurriedly the remaining blocks to the small, timid house where Vivian lived. Through the open door he saw her sitting on the floor reading a book.

"Howdy," he said, walking in without knocking.

"How are you folks?" He moved over to her and touched her shoulder with his knee.

He felt giddy and drunk as a rooster. "Ready to get hitched, gal?"

Now or a year, it wouldn't matter money-wise.

Vivian said, "Whaju say?" There was thrill written on her pretty round face.

"We're getting married tonight," he laughed.

The missus sat over there like a rock, hairpins sticking out of her mouth, and Mr. Galley shoved his neck above his paper like a turtle, wanting to know what they intended to live on.

"I've come into some money…" He didn't know where the words were coming from. The hill and the old shack had flown away like blackbirds.

Removing the hairpins from her mouth, Mrs. Galley asked how in the world he planned to get a license and the preacher at this hour?

"Vivian's friend knows a place," he said experimentally.

Vivian nodded. "Roy knows a place."

"It ain't the way to do things," Mr. Galley was saying behind his paper. "Wait three days for the license the way you're supposed to."

"I'm leaving in the morning."

"Then you can leave my girl behind."

"Daddy," spoke Vivian, "I'm going with him. Even if I have to run off!"

"Frank, you let 'em. It don't do no good to hold young folks back. We knew they'd marry sometime."

The Old Bird asked him how much money he had.

"Hundred dollars," he blurted. He had planned to have a hundred dollars.

"That ain't enough to live on the rest of your life. What do you plan to do?"

"Frank, now! Jale's a hard workin' boy and a hundred dollars is a fine start. You let 'em be. I'll see about the suitcase."

Jale had never told such monstrous lies. He didn't even know whether fourteen dollars was enough money to get married on.

Back in the kitchen he pushed her against the wall and said, "Are you sure? No place to live!"

"Yes, darling," she cried. "Yes!" And she kissed his chin.

He kissed her on the mouth and said, "All right then. We'll do it! We'll do it!"

When they wheeled into the preacher's driveway, Jale felt suddenly as though he had swallowed a toad that he had to get rid of before it choked him to death.

He pushed Vivian against an acacia tree and blurted, "I lied about that hundred dollars. I only had what the license cost. I haven't even got a ring!"

Vivian played with one of the buttons on his green shirt. He stared at her hair so he wouldn't see how beautiful she was and thought about his Old Man that had set out with nothing but the hill. Things did grow good up there where nobody else cared a damn about them raising their eats.

Suddenly he held her face between his hands and asked, "Are you afraid of a hill?"

She laughed. "Why would anybody be afraid of a hill?"

"That's what I say! At least not our big old Chocolate Hill. It's the only free place and it will grow anything. Like being on top of the world!"

Oh, was he glad he had guts. And it was the very reason he loved Vivian. She had guts or she wouldn't have come like she did.

Who said you couldn't get married during the Depression—if you had guts!

CHAPTER 3

I LOVE THOSE INDIANS
(Published by Marshall Jones Company, 1991)

FOREWORD

Rosemary Macklem, formerly of Cleveland, Ohio, has been written up many times in national newspapers with statements such as her single-handed help of as many as 25,000 impoverished American Indians on sixteen reservations in the West.

She has been doing this since 1955. It started when she was on a vacation and stopped at a roadside inn and discovered Indian children digging in garbage cans and an investigation led her to the discovery of the rank poverty of these first American citizens.

Even now, allowed to leave, the Indians stay cooped up on reservations because if they leave, they forfeit their land. Rosemary has known mothers who boiled moccasins for three days to feed their children.

In her 35 years' work Rosemary also has seen real progress from the standpoint of the Indians' resentment of the white man.

It is believed by those who know her, that Rosemary herself has done the biggest part in mending the breach of the two races.

She does love those Indians, as the following true story shows.

Note from Rosemary to author:

"I feel that the Holy Spirit inspired you to write it (the book) and it is almost uncanny in parts, as if you made the trips with me."

I LOVE THOSE INDIANS

When I saw Eddy Little Fox holding a rattlesnake, I nearly fainted. I was afraid to move. Rather under my breath I said: "Be careful, Eddy."

Eddy moved the rattlesnake closer to his face. "He's my friend! See?"

I was impelled to turn away. Going to his mother, a local Hopi Indian, I muttered, "Do you see what Eddy is holding?"

"Yes," she smiled. "He's practicing for the snake dance when he grows up. That snake was barely born when he found it."

My frozen heart remembered what I had been told by Chief Red Cloud's son from the Sioux tribe in North Dakota. "Indians have their ways and it's important to abide by them."

So with the steel of an Indian, I abided.

Named The Good Eagle Woman by this son, I found it's the white man that cramps the Indians by belittling the ways of these first citizens, many earning their living from selling Indian crafts. And any white woman who associates with them is an outcast.

In 1955 I stopped at Porkie's Road Stop for coffee.

Slowly sipping, I looked up and saw a beautiful painting.

"Do you paint?" I asked the sleepy Porkie.

He shook his head.

"Who did paint that beautiful mountain scene, the two bucks with their antlers hopelessly hooked? The name looks like Walking."

"Damned Indian. Give to pay eatin' here."

"Is it for sale?"

Opening his eyes, he said: "Waitin' for somebody to offer me a thousand."

Because it likely was a rather high but fair price unaffordable for me, I mused over my cup thinking someone back in Cleveland probably wouldn't hesitate.

"You say the artist lives around here?" I asked.

"Don't live nowhere. Just roams. When he ain't in jail."

"Jail!" I fairly screamed.

"Drunk! Reason you don't never give 'em money!"

I left, determined he had to be found.

All the hatred and penning up was done, I remembered from history books, because at Custer's last stand, every white soldier was slain by the crafty Indians. It brought the final battle that wiped out thousands of the Indians, women and children included. In fact, it was believed that none were left. The few who were could do nothing but accept their defeat and go where they were told.

The thing was, the country had been their country, the whites the invaders.

I dropped off to sleep in my car, thinking this was the time to acquaint myself with these people while in the area.

Waking up with a start, I heard loud yelling. Suddenly two drunks headed directly for my car.

"Hey! Open up! Come go with us to the square dance!"

What if they broke the window? I cringed.

They pounded louder. "Damn you! We gotta have us a woman!"

Suddenly from nowhere appeared another man. "If you guys want your car, you better follow me." He began hooking a tow rope to their car.

The fellows turned and ran after him. "Stop! Stop!"

I saw in the light of Porkie's that he was an Indian.

"Thank you!" I shouted, to which he said nothing.

In the daylight I found out from Porkie when I went in for breakfast, that the Indian's name was Dead Face and he worked at the garage.

"Why are children allowed to go in and out of a saloon?" I asked a child watching me.

"They ain't! And this ain't no saloon! They're after scraps. They even dig around in the garbage out back. Go look for yourself!"

I did go look for myself.

An Indian woman and some children were face down in the garbage cans. When they saw me they ran like terrified animals.

Cleveland had its hungry. But they had welfare. Churches helped. Who helped these Indians, I began to wonder?

Driving along, I couldn't believe how quickly the Badlands disappeared into a world of fertile farms, well-kept buildings with green pastures, rows of crops. How could man think that fencing citizens off to themselves solved any problem?

Suddenly came the thump, thump of a flat tire. Pulling over, I raised up from the jack and saw a truckload of Indians.

"We'll do!"

"Do you know Felix Walking?" I asked as they worked.

Their faces were set, unchanged. Seeing their non-communicating silence was not to be broken, I thanked them and tried to give them a five dollar bill.

"No!" They jumped into the truck and were off.

At the small, beautifully sculptured, old-time Mission building with a bell tower, I found the door open and walked in.

The walls were covered with Felix Walking paintings, all of the fine, living quality I had seen in the fighting bucks.

The priest, a white man, came forth and I said I was looking for Felix. "Do you have any idea where he could be found?"

"Could be anywhere."

"And about Indian children coming in and out of saloons all night looking for scraps. Mothers digging in garbage cans. Something has to be done about this. What can I do?"

His eyes lit up. "Send food, clothing, money for the sick. The list is endless."

"Do I send them to you?"

"Any of the missions. This is the Rosebud reservation, one of twenty or more. Of course you can help."

As I drove on I grew more and more excited. My mother kept urging marriage. But did I want a man, with children, with the whole Indian race so neglected?

Suddenly I saw the tow man. "Hello! I'm the one you saved towing away those drunks."

He said nothing.

"I'm sorry at the way you folks get treated, and if you'll be my helper, I want to help you wonderful people. Please?"

"I help," he said, his face unchanged.

Returning to Cleveland, I determined not only to go back to the Indians the following summer, but I would spend my spare time collecting clothing and food for them, Dead Face my contact!

Later the whole aircraft company began collecting clothing, canned goods, toys, books.

"How do you know he'll not sell the things?" someone asked.

"I know. That Indian saved my life. When I mentioned to help I saw the deep relief, a hope at last!"

Tom said, "I wouldn't get too friendly with those Tommy Hawkers. Who knows? The scalpers might be after that pretty blonde hair."

"Those Tommy Hawkers saved me from being molested by two white drunks!" I informed him stoutly.

As the winter moved on I found the old car never would hold the load. So I found a U-Haul trailer which could be turned in when empty.

Giving mama a kiss and telling friends to send up a few prayers, I climbed in. Friends yelled and I honked.

Before the day was over the state troopers stopped me. "Where are you taking all this stuff?"

"To the Indian reservations where they walk thirty miles to rummage in garbage cans for food scraps."

He must have believed me for he said, "Good luck!" and rushed forth to catch a speeder.

A few days later I came to a group of trees where ahead I saw a long table, beside which was a bed where an old Indian man lay. When I got out of my car and approached him, I was surprised to see him rise and come to meet me!

I handed him fruit and told him my name.

"Yes." His old, bronze, carved face smiled as he took the things, and he thanked me for my trailer full of things for his people. He said: "The Great Spirit has many ways to bring peace to our family."

I felt in the presence of nobility, a closeness, a mutual understanding and respect that thrilled me.

Finally exhausted, the Chief lay back. He pulled up his trouser leg to show his swollen feet and legs. He said his son took him to the hospital but they wouldn't let him in. "Some white man in hospital. No Indian allowed."

"Some day this will all be changed," I determined.

Before I left I said, "I am looking for Felix Walking, the artist who fills the churches with his paintings."

"Yes, capturing the Great Spirit's beauty. One day you'll find him."

Driving toward a Mission School I saw an Indian woman stumbling along. I stopped, and when I asked her if I could take her somewhere, she said: "I am very sick and going to the hospital." The hospital was eight miles away.

"Please do get in and I'll drive you there!" I said in horror.

It was obvious she didn't think she should. But finally in her despair she did.

"You Good Eagle Woman." She explained that her husband had died and her nine-year-old son was at home alone. "I don't know what to do," she moaned.

When we reached the hospital I told the nurse I found her walking along the road.

"No food," the nurse said. "I can tell by looking at her. It's part of their mourning when their husband dies. What she needs she'll refuse. Vein feeding may or may not save her."

Driving to Rushville where I stopped and asked, "Do you know where I could find Felix Walking?" A man said, to my surprise:

"He's in jail!"

At last! But jail?

Entering the jail I learned that he had been released an hour ago.

"I've been looking for him for over a year!" I moaned.

"That figures. He don't want to be found. That's an Indian for you!"

I moved on in complete defeat. Passing an officer sitting in a car, I asked again.

"He's sitting over there on that bench," the man pointed. "I'm watching to see he don't move."

I walked over and told him about my love for his art. "Your picture of the fighting bucks. I really like that painting. I guess because it seems to represent more than fighting bucks. It would mean a lot to me if you could paint another like that. I would pay."

"No paint."

"How much?"

"Five dollars."

"Here."

His face came alive rather like a starved child offered food.

The sheriff came over. "You get them paints, hear!"

Felix nodded.

Soon mixing colors, his canvas started coming to life.

I was spellbound. He, too, knew it was Indians and whites in conflict he was painting. I felt sure of this.

"You know the struggle between whites and Indians will take time, Felix. But it's bound to resolve. Your paintings help. We're all helping."

It was as though the moment of the resolved conflict had suddenly come.

"It means no more liquor, no more jailings, no time for anything but showing what you can do. Your craft talks."

He said nothing.

"Felix," I began softly, "don't let your people down! I'll do my part. But I can't do it alone. Your art can!"

He raised his head and looked directly at me. There were tears in his eyes. "I ...do," he said huskily.

Back in Cleveland they were amazed as I told where a whole church was jacked up and moved on logs, the death of Mary Hawkwing left to die alone in her death-tent...the pictures Felix Walking had given me to sell.

The following year I stopped at a clearing by a lake to drink in the peace of the trees, birds, of nature. Suddenly, seemingly from nowhere, Harvey Hawknest appeared. "Saw your car. Sent to invite you to Pow Wow."

"That's an honor and I will go!" I said with delight. Indians never ask whites to these rituals.

When I arrived at the clearing set for the Pow Wow, I saw hundreds of Indians already there all bright and bangly with their feathered head-dresses, beads stacked over their deerskin clothing. How plain I looked among them!

They lined up for the Friendship Dance. Mary Little asked me to join in.

It was far more inspiring to watch! There was a dignity about the ritual. One purpose, all one.

"Come back Sun Dance," the feathered Chief came forth and said in his formal manner.

Later I learned that the Sun Dance is very sacred. To be invited was the greatest honor they could bestow on a white person.

When I was back at Chief Red Cloud's son's cot under his favorite tree, I was greeted by his getting up and he said, "Every night we say the Rosary and pray God take care of Rosemary and the President of the United States."

I laughed but wished I hadn't. "So much to learn," I moaned.

"Earth for learning," he pronounced.

Told the Gildersleeves were looking for me, I went on and was horrified to learn that Felix was in the hospital.

"What's the trouble?"

"Drink got him. He die soon."

As I drove as fast as the car and trailer would go, I prayed to God to give me the right words to say.

When I saw his wasted body, I was horrified.

"Felix Walking! You can not lie there waiting to die. Our country needs you. Those paintings to prove Indian people have great talents and must be freed that we can be one nation indivisible!"

He stared at me.

"Don't you remember, Felix? Death isn't going to unite us. Your paintings are! I sold all you sent and here's the money." I handed the wad to him.

No response.

"I am going to get paints and canvas and stay here till you finish every painting my people ordered!"

Returning later, I found him unchanged.

I put up the easel. "One lady wants a mountain scene with a deer and its fawn."

He sighed, turned away.

"Felix, my dear. Don't give up! Try!"

He moaned. "Indian die."

After a long wait, convinced I was not going to leave, he stared at the canvas.

Weak though he was, slowly a clearing vision became a faint reality.

A nurse came in. "What's going on here?"

It was four days later when I returned and gathered up the paintings and left. Felix was with me in the car.

"I have arranged for you to stay at the Mission for a while. According to the nurse, we're the victor."

After leaving him in the loving hands of the nuns, I thought Sister Serena with rules, prayers, and patience would indeed win.

To live in the West was all I could think of as I returned once more to fill my job at the Airplane Factory.

"Mama, you know—have said often—some day I'll move out there."

"Oh, God. Married to an Indian."

"Mama, I hate to disappoint you, but I'm not a bit interested in getting married. Never have been."

"Thank goodness!" mama moaned, to which we both laughed, Indian blood in the old Macklem family?

I had bought the authentic ceremonial clothes the Indians had loaned me for the Pow Wow and Sun Dance, and thought it would be the very thing to walk into the U.S. Director of Indian Affairs to give them a chance to say, "No, we can't help to the extent you ask."

"If not, Mr. President, here I come!"

No good American would put up with the Indians having to walk twenty miles to get their water out of an irrigation ditch because it was against the law to drill for water. (In case they found oil and it being their land they could keep it!)

I was told, "I can't believe such a law still exists. Yet, I'm sure it does or you wouldn't be here."

The story appeared the next morning.

When I left, I had permission to have two drinking-water wells drilled.

"When you get to Phoenix, you will find a letter of permission to present to the officials."

Then came the seemingly unsolvable cow problem. The Treeland Convent was wanting to help a convent's reservation by donating twenty cows. Since feeding and watering would be necessary on the long journey, the cost would be high. "It won't be easy. But they need the cows! Actually, to survive. We have the cows and must send them."

"Oh, my. How could I ask my dear Cleveland friends to come up with, say, three thousand dollars? Trained horsemen, wagons, feed, sleeping quarters, water..."

Driving along slowly, half annoyed with such a big problem tossed in my lap and yet knowing with all those undernourished Indians it must be done, I prayed. "God help me."

I passed a Hollywood sign.

There was the answer! Some rich Hollywood movie star wanting publicity.
I put an ad in the local newspaper, and waited.
Soon I got some calls. Was there a way to prove the authenticity of the project?
I called Sister Ann. Prayed about what else to do.
At last the agent assured me the money would be sent.

Talking about the Indians, I said I had seen squaws build tepees, a circle of poles with buffalo hides sewn together, an opening at the top for smoke from their dirt-floor fires, always facing east as a religious ritual for facing the sunrise. Every need they provided themselves. William said when there were buffalo they fared well. The only weapons they owned were bows and arrows. The Chief's son of Red Cloud said Custer wanted to destroy these Indian Nations, but the Little Big Horn battle killed the entire seventh cavalry.

Then the government wanting to protect the gold mines, made an agreement with the Chief in which his people were placed in reservations, under government control with government aid and protection…but little ever came of any help, the Chief's son said.

As I drove along I was pleased to see a few more wells dug, at last!

"I gotta live out here," I said aloud as I drove along on my homeward journey.

Mama said, "All you think about is the Indians. I really believe you *would* move out there and stay!"

"Mama, you're right. Would you move out with me?"

"Never."

One day out of the blue, money came from a contest I had entered. I went around thanking God at every breath. "Who says there isn't a God looking after you!" Oh, joy of joys! It was like a gift straight from Heaven!

I asked Father Price: "WHY don't whites like Indians?"

"Same reason some whites don't like blacks."

"It seems to me it's time we whites did a little thinking. One day we'll die and go to Heaven. Then what? I bet my last dollar God's not going to segregate us.

Now a Westerner in a house trailer, I was not only a resident but a taxpayer. I was told I could do some teaching. Pleased, I was assigned the Lukachuki area. My work was to teach the Indian women how to budget the tiny money available, along with teaching them personal cleanliness, cooking, and sewing.

Even though I was a light blonde, I was immediately accepted as The Good Eagle Woman. One old Indian man said, "Rosemary, if you get two Navajo Indian women working together, I'll eat my hat."

Within a week I had fifty-four in my class. Soon they were not only making their own camp dresses, but children's clothes and men's shirts and underwear.

The need was always for big sizes. It was the build of the Indian women, rather one fitting all.

I was told in alarm about an Indian woman who had been lying on the floor in labor for three days.

Childbirth was one thing I knew nothing about, but I could drive her to the hospital.

There was a shortcut. Suddenly a huge rock loomed before us. The impact was so great that I cried, "Oh, God, I've killed her!"

Then came the cry of a baby.

When we reached the hospital, I opened the back door and there sat the mother holding her baby.

I often think about little Steve John and how it took a huge rock to shake him into the world.

Finally I caught on to the fact that Indians use their lips as a way of communicating. In a kissing manner they point when giving directions. Thinking back, I realized their stony silence may have given me lip answers.

Finally falling heir to a spaghetti machine, I put the flat dough in, and out came spaghetti to hang on the clothesline to dry. It was not too hard to serve as many as 3,000 Indians in one afternoon. It took two cases of tomato soup, chopped green pepper, onions, and thirty pounds of ground beef.

At first they were dubious, then came back for more helpings.

Water forever a scarcity, the women carried the water from the cooked spaghetti home in pots balanced on their heads, pleased and full for once.

My first Christmas in the West was a magic that spread excitement in spite of blizzards and struggle. With the huge shipments from Cleveland, California, Chicago, even Maryland, there was enough for all. I struck out for the tribes to the north, so long neglected with my teaching job.

"Red Cloud, you're stronger!" I found.

Later I ran into Felix Walking. He gave me a painting of a big, beautiful brown bear and two cubs. I said, "You make them look so gentle."

"Animals not vicious. If they know you like," he stated flatly.

One day I saw a milk truck and asked, "Can you tell me why a quart of milk costs Indians seventy-five cents and for us it's thirty-nine cents?"

"It's the storekeeper that makes the difference," he frowned.

He must have told the retailers, for the next time I wanted to buy something nobody would wait on me. I was understanding how the Indians felt, I that Indian lover.

"Why should I be upset with God on my side?" I was too busy in my year-around work. Right now there were the sheep which were very much a part of these loving people. They cared for them as tenderly as they did their children. The shepherd gave his commands and the goats seemed to take him as a loving parent for all!

One day the Medicine Man came and said they wanted to have a "Sing for the Good Eagle Woman."

"Oh, I'm in fine health," I laughed.

He said, "It gives you protection from the evil spirits."

So Saturday I had my Sing in Rock Feather's hogan. The dedicated doctor chanted to the evils including wolves, bears, foxes, sickness, and even from man's evils.

When the long ceremony was over and I realized the real concern of all these friends, I was deeply moved. For me, we are truly one nation. And if all Americans knew Indians as I do they would be horrified that so many of our Nation's finest people are often hungry and penned up like cattle.

For a long time I had dreamed of having my own clinic with visiting doctor volunteers who would come on a monthly basis. I was going to start one with the contest money.

I slipped off to California to line up volunteers. At a meeting called by my aunt where I was staying, she introduced me as "America's Indian angel of mercy." I told about the baby born in my car, Chief Red Cloud's swollen legs, bad sores on the feet of children I had been saving.

There was dead silence...

I told about going to Washington to plead for water, about the marvelous artist, Felix Walking who had waited to die, my first encounter where mothers and children were digging in garbage cans for anything at all they could find to eat, including cardboard that had held hamburgers.

When I finished someone clapped and others followed. Then a graying man who was a doctor said he would be willing to help a week a year.

Others followed. The clinic became a reality, ending up with thirty volunteers.

I had a spaghetti dinner and more than 3,000 Indians came. I informed them of the free clinic and gave them schedules as to when doctors and nurses would be available.

Suddenly I had the most overwhelming wave of peace I had ever had in my life. It came from what Martha had said about waiting on God.

I thought of Ira Hayes, the Indian Marine who helped raise the U.S. flag on Mt. Suribachi in Iwo Jima. He died in 1955 begging for his people's help. He didn't want a Purple Heart, he wanted one thing: water for his people.

I drove to see Ira Hayes' parents who lived in a one-hundred-year-old adobe on the Pima reservation. Joe Hayes, Ira's father, was dead, and the boys went to the mountains to bring back driftwood to sell so the family would have enough to eat. Grown, they came looking for candy.

"Joe, how would you like to go to the Vocational School and learn a trade?"

Eating a caramel, he said he would like that.

"How about you, Kenny?" I asked.

His face didn't change but he nodded.

"Then come and we'll give you the training." When I left I thought, "Ira, you got what you wanted. A trade for your brothers."

I drove to the Mission School. Sister Serena came shouting,

"Rosemary! They have taken everything out of your trailer and there is nothing left!"

"What do you mean? Who?"

"Stolen!"

I immediately called the sheriff at Gallup.

"What was stolen?" he asked calmly. "Make a list. Who told you?"

When I finally reached my trailer I was told by the Indians that the thieves had even taken my spaghetti machine.

I felt as if I had been clubbed near death. All I had to my name were the clothes on my back.

When the sheriff and a couple of men came they stood and laughed.

"Well! Looks like you've been grounded!"

I got in the car and drove as fast as I could. All I could think of was that this had been done by my own people. Indian haters.

Finally I stopped. Life seemed over.

I looked down on the children having recess. Hadn't I been warned enough, gas shut off so pipes froze. My people were at war with the Indians and I was an Indian. I broke into sobs. Not even a toothbrush...

Mother mustn't know.

Was it right to steal?

I knew I had to get on the highway and move in a straight line to Aunt Peg's in Hollywood.

"You were the only one I felt I could turn to."

"Well, we know you can't go back. But don't forget you have helped the Indians for more than twenty years. Rosemary, it's time you quit."

In a few days I decided to go to San Francisco to stay with relatives, Aunt Jewel, where I would have an address. There were friends, Mother, who would be concerned if I dropped out of existence the way I wanted to.

I could put an ad in the paper and get a little money out of my trailer till I found a job.

"Yes," I told mother. "All's fine. Just wanted to let you know I'm finally visiting Aunt Jewel. You okay?"

"Okay as can be expected."

From mama, that meant all was well.

It was suddenly as though mama was right. What good of it all?

The word got out about my theft.

"Well! That's a lot of thanks! I've heard Indians steal—"

"Not Indians!" I screamed. "White Indian haters! Who include me as an Indian!"

As various people asked me about Indian crafts, Pow Wows, the Trade School, I was asked to speak before a group and my old love and enthusiasm came back. I couldn't believe I'd walked off and left it all. Someone said, "Here's a hundred

17

dollars for the Trade School."

A neighbor said, "Let's give a party and collect toys, clothes, canned food, cash."

I ended up having to rent another U-Haul.

"Keep in touch!" my aunt called as slowly I took off.

When I returned to the clinic, I was handed a telegram. Mother was gravely ill, facing leg amputation.

My neglect of mother came like an avalanche.

Vivian was the one person I knew would be able to take over the clinic, so I asked her to look after shipments and whatever else might come up. "My mother's sick and I have to leave at once!"

"Don't worry about a thing," came Vivian's sweet, assuring voice.

At long last, here I was in Cleveland, good old Frank to meet me.

Mother had had a shot for arthritis and had a bad reaction.

"You have to expect things like this," he said.

Immediately I began a twenty-minute interval of saline solution.

"Sip a little of this Indian tea."

"Oh, God," mama groaned. "Not that!"

I had the feeling mother would recover with no loss of limb. What a reward for my years in the West with my Indians, I suddenly realized!

Days flew. Who could believe it had been two months! In my spare time, I had given talks here and there, talked to reporters, and with much anticipation, went back to visit my friends at the Aircraft Company. They had a little after-work party for me, all ears about my new clinic, the baby being born in the car, Felix.

"What I wish is that you would come see these proud Americans we pushed off to lands we didn't want—too unproductive to eke out a living. We need their stamina, their philosophy."

It was a few days later when Vivian called and said, "Rosemary, something's going on you need to know about. You need to come. I mean this!"

When at last I was face to face with Vivian I couldn't believe my ears.

Someone announced on the radio, "Has anyone seen a lady named Rosemary Macklem who claims she's helping the Indians and no Indian has ever heard of her?"

The Indians' silence was backfiring on me.

Calling, I said, "I am Rosemary Macklem. Please announce that I have had to go to Cleveland because of my sick mother, but now I am back to continue my 20 years' work here with the American Indians."

Waiting for the broadcast, *I was shocked to hear the plea repeated.*

I drove to the station and sighted a reporter and unloaded.

He smiled. "An Indian came in here and said, 'I know Rosemary Macklem and you better watch out! Not an Indian that doesn't know The Good Eagle Woman!'"

The next day the paper carried a rebuttal explaining how I had helped thousands of Indians with food, medical needs, clothing, cooking classes. The article couldn't have helped but wipe out the smear. A politican said, "I guess you're helping the Indians too much; being one of them is not acceptable, I've found."

One day at the clinic Dr. Worley said: "Why have we been so long learning of these critical needs of the Indians?"

I looked at him. "Dr. Worley, has any Indian said more than two words to you? Have they said anything, except to answer a direct question?"

He smiled. "No, I should have known. Do they not want us to know about their plight?"

"They accept help, meekly. We should have known without having to be told that the losers shoved into the Badlands would have a hard time surviving."

"You're right."

CHAPTER 4

HAVE A CUP OF BYGONES
(Published by The Golden Quill Press, 1982)

'Twas Saturday. Crops were in and up.
As the pile of cowchips used for fuel
In the range and pot-bellied stove was gone,
Papa hitched the horses to the wagon
And they all climbed in to replenish the heap.

When the slow team stopped folks jumped and scattered.
Chips had no smell and the fibrous substance
Made from pasture grazing was dry and firm.
Except for shape, resembled driftwood.
By the old gray look one knew what to pick.

Chips burned bright like twigs and long like stumps,
Kept a family warm and cooked its food.
Ample, handy, and ever replaced,
Answered the prayers of the pioneers.
(Maybe even some day answer the world's!)

BEAVER'S FIRST CAR

Doctor Long had a beautiful team
Of roans that he hitched to his buggy
And drove to the country farms day or night
With a speed no one else could equal.

The first horseless carriage ne'er 'fore seen,
They were more worried than proud as he
Hurried along at the terrible speed
Of fifteen miles an hour no less.

He's the king of the town and knows it.
Some day he'll hit someone and then what?
Cause a runaway team—kill more'n one.
Well, at least the doctor would be there!

THE TOP OF PIKE'S PEAK

After mama died papa reached a day
When he said they were driving to Pike's Peak.
When he left Law School and went West with his chum
With the plan to find a place to settle,
They saw the high mountain but thought their bikes
Would be destroyed on the long, rocky road.

"I never lost my desire to climb it,
Stand at the top and view the whole wide world.
It'll be a way to keep my head straight."
Aunt Margaret was still with them then,
So bedding, food, clothes, were loaded
And atop the Model T newly bought.

Came a day when papa said, "See that cloud?"
A cloud in the hot, pale, gray-blue sky?
"Straight ahead, just above the horizon.
That's Pike's Peak. That's your first view of it."
His voice broke in a sob of joy and pain.
'Twas something he'd promised to show his Dee.

Now and then they had to unload and push,
With always the horror of tumbling down
Hundreds of ever-mounting feet below.
Then they reached the Lodge where people parked.
'Though hot below there was blizzarding snow
'Round the Lodge, no one dressed for the cold.

Here atop the crowd stared in silent awe.
Every direction the eye saw no end.
In the West the sky was a brilliant splash
Of fiery colors beyond human guess.
"Your mother's out there in all that beauty,"
Papa gasped with a catch in his throat.

The little toy train winding its way
At the bottom of the Royal Gorge,
Its smoke but a whiff of cloud above, is
Where they stood looking down a mile.
Since papa had grown up with sisters
He had mastered the art of teasing.

*To get a rise he started picking
With care, his way down the mile-deep gorge.
"John Alva Spohn, your mind has left you.
Don't you know you could slip? Stop! Fool!"
It was what he expected and laughed.
What he was not expecting was Bess.*

*She screamed in terror ne'er before heard.
"Papa! Papa!" People rushed forth.
"What's happened! Has someone fallen!"
Red-faced, he made his way back up.
"Man! One slip and you'd fed the bears!"
"Papa's here. Nothing to cry about!"*

*On they traveled homeward, O anxious
For the wide empty span of prairie
Where the windmill sang and cattle grazed
And little kittens scampered about.
Papa cried to see the lonesome house.
"You had your dream, John, you had your dream."*

A BROKEN ARM

*Papa was inventive…fixed some crates
To deliver separated cream
And milk to customers in town,
All neatly stacked in the Model T.*

*It was the daily job of Hugh and Jean.
Papa had bought a herd of Holsteins,
Black and white cows with a handsome bull.
The boys and grandpa milked while papa*

*Proudly ran the cream separator,
A machine that separated cream
From milk by the turn of a crank.
Grandma hated the thing because papa*

*Made sure every disk, tube, and bowl was
Washed in suds, scalded and set to sun;
Even so, the great contraption smelled
of cows in that part of the kitchen.*

One night when the car was loaded full
Of the bottles and caps papa'd bought
(Which had to be washed and scalded, too)
The boys started off, Jean at the wheel.

It was choir practice night at the church
So May, papa and Bess walked the mile.
They were singing along when the Sheriff
Rushed in and said Hugh'd broken his arm.

"Broke his arm?" Papa said, singing stopped.
"Cranking the car as you might have guessed,"
Said the Sheriff, gasping for breath.
"I'm surprised you didn't hear him yell!"

"How can a crank break an arm?" one asked.
"Let go and sometimes the dang thing spins.
Better get yourself free of the crank
Or it'll hit you like a bullet."

He had become a hero of sorts.
"Hugh Spohn broke his arm cranking the car."
"It'll happen, I tell you. Bet your life.
Old crank'll kick like a mule. Lord, Lord."

WET FEATHERS

Seldom do the plains have heavy rains,
So when they come, they're unexpected.
Even a hen with her new hatched brood
Can't cope with the rain's sudden rivers.

So over the yard float baby chickens
Drowned you would think from their lifelessness.
But gathered in a basket, grandma
Would wrap them in a flannel blanket

And put them in the cookstove oven
Until one by one they popped to life,
Loud cheep-cheeps e'er bugs to chase and eat.
And where was their big clucking mama?

When the sun burst forth and dried the yard
Grandma took her basket of cheepers
Back to the desolate mother hen,
Feathers of love and joy united!

PRIMING THE WINDMILL PUMP

The stillness was strange, even frightful.
For days the wind had ceased its blowing.
On the prairie the wind was a friend.
Water for washing, cold drinks for the thirsty.

"Get out the old milk cans and we'll haul
Enough to drink and fill the horse tank.
Some strange death of wind had struck the land.
Then hiss rattle bang. The wind, the wind!

Papa got up and lit the lantern
To see if the windmill was pumping.
He returned to ask grandma for water.
"Pump's lost its prime. Take, say, a gallon."

Down the pipe that led to the water.
Pump pump went the windmill, not a drop.
"Come on, come on!" Papa yelled. "Come on!"
Then a trickle…the smallest trickle.

How sweet the wind, rocking trees, singing
Buoyant songs through window cracks, aye,
Providing cold, constant water.
Who ever can object to the wind?

BLAZES IN THE NIGHT

*On the fourth of July the rockets
Burst o'er Beaver in a blaze of glory!
Back when town-made hose carts rushed to fires
With little hope of saving a house,
A glimpse of fire in the big frame school
Where a rocket lay on its shingles
Was at once a sight of ghastly doom.
What could save the pride of the prairie?*

*People screamed and rushed in a torrent
With only the thought of saving books,
Saving desks and records—school records!
Athletes risked their lives to save
The desks where their initials were carved,
The pickled snakes, the Beaver Pennants.
The heap of burning rubbish laid a grave
To determined, high aiming townsmen.
The unfinished Baptist Church made room
For school till a building could be built.
But what skimping, skimping—years to come!*

CHAPTER 5

HE THINKS TREES THINK
(From The Chocolate Hill, *Published by The Golden Quill Press, 1994)*

Everybody thought old Asop Green was nuts. "There goes old Asop Green, the nuttiest man in town. He thinks trees think," a guy said.

"What do they think?" I asked and thought, "O how nutty it would be To read a poem by a tree."

People were turning around and gawking at me and I was losing sight of old Asop Green, so I chucked the poetry and concentrated on following the nut.

It wasn't his thinking trees think that made me think he was a nut; after all, who was I to say whether trees think or not? Being twenty doesn't mean I know everything. In fact, there are quite a few things I don't know.

I thought old Asop was nuts because of the way he was rigged out. For trousers he had on a pair of golf pants that looked as though he had found them in a pile of junk somebody had dumped out for the Salvation Army, and he had on an old brown coat fastened with safety pins. On his head was one of those jungle hats. Funny thing about his face, it was brown and wrinkled.

It must have been over a mile before the nut stopped. He untied the gunny sacks on his feet and stepped up to a pepper tree.

I almost bumped into him and let on like I was looking for a stray cow.

"COW!" he yelled. "Did you say COW?"

"I thought—it was a—cow," I ventured, feeling my way along, remembering the fella was the nuttiest man in town.

"I wouldn't want cows in here. Not cows!"

"I don't guess it was a cow," I hastened.

Then he eyed me sharply. "Was it a horse? Goat? Pig?"

"I don't guess it was anything." And then I asked him if he had something inside that tree making a noise, or *why* was he holding his ear up against the trunk that way? "Like put-put or tick-tick?"

"Trees don't putput, they hum." And he asked me, did I ever hear a tree hum? When I shook my head he said:

"Trees think. Have brains the same as people. Take this grove, I set out every tree and from the first day I talked to them as if they were my children."

"Huh," I said, astounded.

He told me to come and stick my ear against Edith and listen to her hum.

I did and didn't hear a thing.

He said, "You want to speak to her like a gentleman." Then he said,

"Edith, I want you to meet a new friend, like me. Mr., Mr…"

"Hicks," I said.

Not a sound.

All of a sudden he looked down at my feet. "You've got shoes on!"

"Sure. I ain't no barefoot boy."

"Take the shoes off. She's got to have feet against her roots."

"I'm beatin' it," I said. "Gotta look for my..."

Old Asop crumpled up like a dog I'd hit and was leaving there to die.

"Oh, Hicks! A tree in this greedy, indifferent, unbelieving world is like a beautiful queen in a den of thieves, with her only weapon her dignity, grace, and quiet beauty which she holds to the end."

"Amen," I yelled, egging him on.

"Have you ever watched a man chop a tree? Trees love us! Love to have us throw our arms around them. So now come over here and tell Edith you care. Come before I lose patience."

I gazed at him through my fingers. I might have to get up and run.

He looked like I was his last straw. Like Mom when she tried to get me to 'go forward' at church and be saved.

I put my ear against the tree and listened. "What's that buzz?"

"That's Edith, Hicks, she's talking to you!"

I pulled my head away. There wasn't any buzz. I went to another tree named Gideon and said, "Gideon, can you hum like Edith?"

The same soft hum. Inside the tree! "Paula, Kate, Obadiah...Do you hear me? Do you honest to God think?"

A queer rusty sound as if she would talk if she knew how.

Asop wept. His joy was boundless.

Discovering trees think is nothing to be put under a basket. The whole world should know.

But everything's gone against me. Mom thought I'd had a sunstroke and my Old Man wanted to put me in the nut house.

It's not for me, you don't have to believe me. The least you can do is give them a hug.

Can you imagine living on earth without trees?

WORK HORSE

Up until Odessa Vance was nineteen, she plowed out in her father's long black-soiled fields in southern Iowa. She'd been proud of perching up on the high metal seat behind old Star and Queen, cultivating the sweet new-earth-smelling ground. She was proud of being her papa's only boy, her papa's work horse, as he called her.

But ever since she had won that thousand dollars for having the prettiest eyes in the contest, plowing was something she thought she should hide away in her desk drawer.

It was when she saw Jane Bowls swinging her fur coat and acting as though she, the Work Horse, didn't exist that Odessa wanted to be different.

She hated life. Jane flunked most of her classes but there was something sort of refined and lady-like about flunking. Although it would be different if she herself flunked. At home she would be in shame, school too, no doubt.

If Jane got in trouble it didn't bother her a bit. She had blonde hair and long curled lashes, and her eyes were a light gray-blue. It made Odessa wish hers weren't such a blue blue.

One day a teacher, Mr. Benton, came up to her and said, "I would like to see you in my office after school. Come to my office, please."

She was scared. She didn't fit anywhere but on the farm helping papa. Never would she be anything but papa's work horse! So what now?

Standing inside the door of his classroom she saw the walls were covered with pictures which made it look more inviting than scary.

The lean Mr. Benton told her in his slow way to have a chair. There was only the one beside his, so she sat down, self-conscious, and didn't know what to do or say. It was like the time papa got mad and sent her looking for a job.

"I like your eyes," he said bluntly.

She was shocked.

"So I think I'll paint them, if you don't mind."

She didn't know what to say so she said nothing.

He moved to help her take off her coat. "Better take your gloves off, too," he said.

"I don't think I will," she said, embarrassed.

"Why not?" Benton stopped short, puzzled.

"Well, I've got—'dishpan hands'."

Benton threw back his head and laughed so hard Odessa was horrified.

He said, "I never have seen dishpan hands. Let me take a look."

He was making fun of her and she hated him and started for the door like a hornet.

Benton grabbed her arm. "Miss Vance, I can't tell you how sorry I am! I want to get a painting of your eyes. They're so blue."

"You'll probably die in the attempt," she stated, so horrified she felt choked.

"Oh, come now. I have everything all set. It's going to be the best picture I ever have painted. Maybe I will win the big prize. Wouldn't it please you to see your portrait hanging up in the art building? Everybody exclaiming over it? Now, wouldn't it?"

She thought about Jane. That would show her *she* wasn't such a queen.

She walked slowly back to the chair. But she would not take off her gloves.

Benton sat at his easel and begged her not to move.

Odessa let her thoughts wander back to the farm. Mama and papa would be sitting by the stove in the kitchen reading their Bibles. The kitchen would smell of sauerkraut and cured ham and wood smoke coming from the big old cookstove.

Tiger, the big soft striped cat, would be curled up asleep in the dent of Mama's lap.

Hot, she removed her gloves.

Professor Benton said, "Better stop. It's getting late. Come back tomorrow after school. Wear the same blue dress."

The cold stung her thin stockinged legs and made her wish she had on her boots. She wished for *something* that was herself, not the pretense of trying to fit into this life. She didn't fit in anywhere but at home on the farm!

One day Jane stopped her and said, "Have you seen your picture?"

"No," Odessa blushed.

"Better go take a look. It's in the art room on exhibit."

Odessa felt smothered. She covered her burning face with her hands and was afraid to look.

"Oh, God, help me!" she fought tears.

The Hands! The Hands! They lay large and dishpanny in her lap, the blue making them worse. She saw not a streak of refinement in the whole thing. She looked exactly the way she felt—big, crude, unrefined. The artist had even caught the surging timidity within her.

It was her out in the cornfield where she belonged.

Someone touched her arm. It was the artist.

"It won the national prize," he bragged. "And it has a handsome price tag."

Odessa stood awkwardly. "The hands," she managed finally.

"How did they get that way?"

"I—well, I help papa plow and shuck corn," she said defiantly. "I'm a farm girl and proud of it!"

"It gives you a beauty no other way found," he stated. "Just being one's true, honest self is always beautiful."

Odessa felt relief in her heart. Never again did she need to wish she could be like Jane.

CHAPTER 6

THE REMINDING WIND
(Published by Naylor Company., San Antonio, TX, 1967)

The wind, the wind, what a tale
It has to tell of the wide and empty
Prairie, with its cottonwoods
That sip along the edge
Of a long and winding creek,
Where the killdees cry
And sail above the sandhills
To join the hot and cloudless sky!

'Twas in the early nineteen hundreds
When a man of remarkable courage
Dreamed of greatness for the prairie
Called the land of Oklahoma
In the narrow Western Strip.
He saw the room to grow,
To soar, to contemplate,
And somehow never cease to know

That God wanted stout men here,
To make an undeveloped land
A little freer, a little richer,
In simple human worth.
The challenges were keen.
How in the world would a man succeed
Unless the Lord God above
Supplied all the things he would need!

A man should have a woman, and he
Knew the girl he wanted most.
She'd love the buttercups, bobolinks, and the
Fields of blooming yucca with their spired bells.
She'd love the sunflowers frolicking in the wind
Like children free to play.
It would be easy here, he thought, for a
Woman who'd long been taught to pray.

So he married her, and they built a house of sod
And joined the one little country church.
Talented in music, she loved the fertile spaces
And filled them all with song.
Teaching the young and old, she traveled in a buggy
With the world's most handsome mare.
The air was filled with Beethoven and Brahms,
Because of her need to share.

The Indians and the buffalo had given up,
Parting in peace, 'though the land
Was the only portion of the Nation that had
Never been made a state. It was free to him
Who marked a claim and hauled his water,
And grew what all he could,
With prairie chicken meat
And chips of cattle dung in place of wood.

The blizzards sent their stinging sleet
And the summers scorched the plains,
While the years brought children, three.
And the wind refused to cease.
"Well, all right, let's harness the fighting fool!"
They dug a well through months of struggle and strain,
And built a towering windmill that sang forever
A loud and happy-go-lucky refrain.

Primroses and whiskered purple thistles
Hid rabbits with ears the size of a donkey's.
And prairie-dog towns came to life in all directions,
As wagons loaded with ranchers lumbered past
To spelling bees and auction suppers,
Or a mere exchange of plants and seeds,
So deep and spurring were the friendships
Dredged by the prairie man's basic human needs.

Then the land became a state. The man
Was a lawyer, so on the builders moved
To Beaver where the people were lining up
For the peace that they themselves had seen.
Let's take the Nation's uncontaminated part
And keep the flowers, keep the neighboring trails.
Keep it lawful from the very start.

The battle was for growth, to make a people strong,
Enduring sickness, death, and wind that filled the eyes
With sand that covered up the crops.
They brought doubts that the mourning doves
Knew well could never be overcome.
So far from home! cried the pioneer women's hearts
Like a ceaseless, far-away drum.

The man with his law got elected
To the county post of judge.
From his farming to his office
His heart was filled with wonder
At this road to his highest aim in life.
His prairie was marching with the Nation's history,
And the town adored his gentle-natured wife.

Ah, the man's music-making woman
Kept a-hearing in the wind,
"You'll never see the loves of home again."
The coyotes sang it
With the sobbing mourning doves.
And the wind around the windows moaned and sighed.
"I don't know why I feel so weak, so sick."
Then in the fullest bloom of life, she died.

Ah, the man had made a promise
To help to build a land.
So on and on he struggled, till the elements
Gnarled and twisted him like a tree.
He was faithful to the end
To his principles of good.
His children off, he might have gone himself,
Yet he wouldn't if he could.

So with trials in court and friends to counsel
The man gave all he had.
When the compromising few
Were bound to get him out,
He knew his Shakespeare, knew his Bible,
Knew his Nation's laws,
And he had his chance again,
To whittle at his county's many flaws.

*The Nation sagged with its Depression
And another siege of war.
But disasters were nothing new;
And the pioneers more than did their part,
Knowing if all the men in all the world
Had given and tugged as hard as they,
The need for one another
Would carve a better, less hate-bespattered way.*

*The children the man had given up,
So they could find an easier way to the stars,
Were too busy for one who loved them too much
To interfere with their awesome-sounding careers.
Besides, the fragments of a shattered past
Held nothing but tears and anguish
For the young who wanted their visions to last.*

*Now a cattle tank and windmill
Are all that's left to guard the builder's dream.
There's a tumbled 'dobe wall
Where centipedes and rattlesnakes have found a home.
Still the loves of left ones
And descendants who never cease to care
Spread a clinging, tenacious mist
Of memories and prayer.*

*So, sing on, sing on forever,
Oh, wind with your melancholy song.
For these great things everlasting
Are a promising look through an open door.
Rich beyond instruments to measure
Are these lands calling: "Give! Give!"
It's the only way a man of God
Can learn to really live."*

CHAPTER 7

GOD HAVING FUN
(Published by Marshall Jones Company, 1992)

GOD HAVING FUN

Fun-having is a property of man who doesn't take life too seriously in his quest to climb mountains that can't be avoided, like school, taxes.

God made man in His exact likeness (*Genesis 1*).

This true, how can we cringe in thinking of God as fun-loving? How could He have thought up a slow, ponderous elephant, if He hadn't enjoyed the amusing thought? Or a high-stepping ostrich? A wide-eyed hop-toad whose long tongue lazily catches flies…a pig with its cocky ears and snout, along with that grunt like an old man that doesn't listen to his wife's chatter but grunts to make her think he's listening. Bright-winged grasshoppers that spit tobacco.

Oh, my. The firemen who very carefully carried out an old woman buried in covers to find it was the family's pet bird dog. The woman who told her marital problems to the plumber when she thought she had dialed her son.

There is something relaxing in the vision of God not only adoring but enjoying his infinite creation.

Who can not kneel in little-child thanks, or doubt that it would be fun to be God having fun?

THESE MEN

"Has papa hitched yet, Artie? Look and see if papa's hitched. We don't want to go foolin' around and miss out!"

"It don't do no good, mama; he'st goes right on talkin'."

"You go tell him anyway, Artie. Mr. Howe don't want to stand and talk all day if he's going to plow."

Artie took one more lick at the spoon then he shot out the door like a bee out of a bottle.

Serena chuckled, giddy as a girl. She doubted if there was another man in all the Ozarks who would go to an auction to bid on a set of dishes for his wife when he wanted a pig. Always before it had been pigs.

But for so long she had waited for one thing grand to have in her rickety unpainted house with its home-made chairs and beds.

She went to the bedroom to get her old black straw hat that made her look plumb silly with its crown poked up out of shape like a muffin with too much baking powder.

"This tub ready?" Frank yelled.

"Yes, all ready."

"Can I take my niggershooter, mama?"

"Yes, lamby, take your niggershooter, but watch out you don't hit someone or scare the horses."

"Do you think they'll get at the household things first?" she asked as she climbed into the wagon.

"Hogs first," Frank said. "Never heard of 'em gittin' at the house goods first."

"Papa," she began gently, "if you think that shoat's the one you want—" She had gone this long without pretty things. And she did have him and Artie.

"Well, my land, Serena! Do you want 'em or don't you? If you can't make up your mind, I will go ahead and bid on the shoat."

Serena felt choked. "Lovie, of course I do want the dishes, but I just thought..."

"Then I don't want to hear no more. I told you I'd get 'em, didn't I? So now forget it!"

In front of the old weathered house was the furniture waiting to be auctioned. Dressers with the mirrors tipped back as if the tree-tops wanted a look; old women resting in the rockers to be sold as if they, too, were going to go to the highest bidder. On the table with the pitchers and milk crocks Serena saw the dishes waiting.

"Look, papa, they're there!"

Frank snorted and said where did she expect them to be, out with the hogs?

Now that she was here with the dishes exposed to anyone who had the money to bid, Serena got sick with dread. These flower-like jewels were in her hands, but they were too pretty, too fragile for her own ugly cupboard with its knobs made from nails put through spools.

When dinnertime came at last the men, carrying their forks and spoons in their shirt pockets, swarmed around the table piling their plates high. Serena labored giving Artie his gizzard and Frank his back, and the auctioneer his piece of gooseberry pie.

"Frank, town woman in the blue coat's been looking at the dishes."

Frank laughed. "Let 'er look. You don't mind if she looks at yer dishes, do you, Serena?" winking at Bert.

Serena grinned. Nobody ever *had* outbid Frank, once he took a notion.

"Over this way, folks! Household things now 'fore we go back to the barn."

Nobody expected the man to get up and start yelling before the women were through dividing leftovers and sorting their spoons; and even a child would know the men had to have their smokes.

"Tell him to wait a little bit, Cora, for the men. Hardly any of the men are around."

"They'll come trailin' back, soon's the auctioneer gets goin' good."

"And even if they don't, you can bid on the dishes. All you do is stand up and call out your bid."

Serena had never bid in her life, and Frank said there was a knack in speaking out like you meant to keep on forever.

"Artie!" she called. She could hear the loud rattle of the auctioneer who didn't care a button who got what.

"Dollarnaquarterabidabidabid!"

Frank ought to be able to hear that even if he were off somewhere looking at Bert's peanuts... Talking with the stranger in the speckled suit who the women said was trying to get himself elected to Congress.

He was auctioning the bed all of Cora's children had been born in, solid walnut. And there was the town lady saying "Eleven!" like a man.

Frank probably was coming already, maybe stopped behind some tree to light his pipe out of the wind.

"Sold for twonahalf! And now folks, the handsome five-leaf table. Er, first the trinkets. Milk crocks, whada hearon the milk crocks?"

She pushed her way through the crowd. Go to the hog pen! "You haven't seen Frank, have you? It's very urgent!"

"Sold fora dollar! And ladies and gentlemen! Look what we have here! Genuine handpainted dishes, handpainted dishes! Whada hearon these genuine handpainted dishes?"

"Now see there!" Serena screamed. "Didn't I know!"

She groped in the direction of the barn.

Those little cups that she and Artie had pounded nails in the cupboard for were hers!

"Frank!"

"Makitfournafournafour!"

"Four!" she called, a call for her man.

"Step up closer, lady!" he was yelling at her.

"Andahalfahalfahalf!"

"Four an' a half!" she defied the whole world.

The crowd laughed. "No use bidding against yourself, lady!"

Tears rose to Serena's eyes. She didn't know how. The bluebirds were let loose and she didn't know how to save them. "Oh, Frank, I said it wrong!"

The town lady was bidding. Her with her pile of pretty things and her gloves.

"Whatmabidabidabid!"

"Five dollars and fifty cents!" Serena shouted. Those were hers! Frank said! But at the same time calling her bid a new voice that turned Serena cold. Hoke Gibson somebody said was fixing to marry the redhead with the painted cheeks. In a little while the cups would have broken handles and the little bluebirds would be thrown into the slop. Surely Frank wouldn't let the Gibson man beat him *if he were here!*

Well, he'd talked big too many times.

"Six dollars and fifty cents!" she called.

"Seven!" called the town woman.

"Seven-fifty!"

"Nine-fifty!" said Hoke Gibson in his swaggering way.

"Ten dollars!" If Frank couldn't get himself here…

"Ten dollars and fifty cents!" came the immediate response from the town female, yelling like a man.

How could it have crawled up beyond ten so fast? With the Gibson man hardly warmed up? She didn't even know whether Frank had more than ten dollars! Artie would be the one to suffer if she used his money she'd been saving.

"Twelve-twenty-five!" yelled the woman. A sack of flour, sugar, Artie's school books. Such a fool she was. She had no right to those dishes….

The auctioneer's words tumbled down dead. "Sold to the gentleman for twelve-fifty." So her lovely bluebirds were fluttering away.

She saw Frank and Artie coming around the corner of the barn.

"Frank…" She couldn't talk.

"Well, Serenie. What are you blubberin' about?"

"The bluebirds. I didn't know how. And the Gibson man kept a-biddin' 'gainst the town lady. What could I do! Him and his redhead. Money we don't have. . ."

Frank threw his head back and laughed loud and long. Then he said something strange.

"I had Hoke bid on your dishes because I knew *he* could handle the town lady. Them dishes were yours and you were gonna get 'em."

"Me?"

Serena reached down and poked a shock of hair inside Artie's straw hat and tried to think what the words meant.

"Did you hear that, Artie? Did you hear what papa said, baby doll? I bet there isn't a woman in the whole world as happy as your mama. Oh, Frank. Oh, Frank!" It was all she could say.

WHO PUTS THOUGHTS TO BED?

We hear often in this troubled world: "I didn't sleep a wink last night!" And we can tell the person is distraught over the lack of sleep more than what kept him awake.

There is a relieving answer to sleeplessness which does not include sleeping pills nor counting sheep. It is in facing the true need of sleep, that eight hours of man's total inactivity. This is extremely important.

The body needs rest because all day long it has to sit, stand, walk, talk, eat, drive a car, iron a shirt, dial a phone, wash hands, hair, teeth, even reading takes the body activity of eye seeing. No wonder the need for the night's dark is so welcome.

Rest for body is a part of nature's plan like winter for trees, so much so that we may find ourselves going to sleep in our chair!

I was that sleepy one night and as it was bedtime, I welcomed my good old bed, its covers just right and enough fresh air to enjoy the cool, the body positioned for the ultimate of coziness.

I gave a deep sigh. "Oh, boy. This is great." The clock on the stand said 10 p.m. I would be getting up at my usual 6 a.m. for my morning walk and that inspiring glimpse of the stars.

Now in bed my mind was pleasantly exploring in a kind of lazy peace with time now to think about all the wonders of the universe. The oceans, mountains, tiny forget-me-nots, a nest of baby birds...

After a time I looked at the clock and saw that it was midnight. I had lost all my sleepiness and thought this could be another of those sleepless nights. What did it matter? It was only my body that needed the rest, and I was so relaxed and comfortable that I knew I couldn't be more settled for a good night's *rest*.

Did my mind need rest? No, not as long as I didn't fret and stew about being too awake to doze.

So sleepless, I got into the old pattern of thanking the Maker for all His wonders.

"Thank you for health, for friends, for my home, my pets, my car, money that sometimes comes from unexpected places."... There were enough things to be thankful for to last for hours.

I looked at the clock. It was 1:13.

Making sure my body was getting its rest, I went back to musing. (Webster's Dictionary defines musing as: "To ponder, meditate, ruminate.")

I turned thought to the book I was working on, I really did enjoy having a manuscript to harvest some day.

By now it was five o'clock.

"I think I'll get up."

My dog and cat are always ready for the new day to start.

So off we went.

"I feel as rested as if I had slept the whole night through," I found in the cool morning air.

So the next time you can't sleep, remember it's the body, not the mind, that needs those hours of inactivity.

Leaving disturbed thoughts out keeps us undisturbed, rested!

WHAT KNEES ARE MADE FOR

Have you ever wondered about your knees? So bendable, so well padded? They're just the long-accepted part of our perfectly designed being with its head, eyes, nose, ears, mouth with teeth for chewing, along with our digestive system, heart, lungs, etc.

Knees must have been made especially for kneeling in thanks to our infinite God Creator for everything from our loves, to stars to wheat supplying grain for bread.

Have you noticed when you do kneel you find a nice flat surface, the position very comfortable?

Our Father God seems to say: "I love you, my son. Look to Me as your close unseen Friend that cares for you far more than any human can."

The full reality of being in this presence of our divine creator does seem to come in the kneeling. So long it has been a means of expressing worship, paying homage.

Life is an amazing experience. There is little more one can ask of Him Who must enjoy Himself making us joyful.

The whole universe with its tall redwoods, little baby bears, kittens.

No wonder in the awe of it all we need knees for kneeling.

He created corn that pops, husbands that snore, old hens that cackle, and cows that expel dung that when dry can be tossed in national cow-chip tossing contests…tender compassionately inspiring little birds that build nests, dogs to pull families out of burning homes.

Who can ask more out of life? Who can not kneel in wistful, little child thanks?

God knew very well we would need knees. When we're overflowing with gratitude for His continual flow of countless blessings!

CHAPTER 8

THE NONCONFORMING PROFESSOR
(Published by Marshall Jones Company, 1988)

THE NONCONFORMING PROFESSOR

William Meese Newton was born November 4, 1907 in Dallas, Texas. His parents, Harry and Maude Newton, were in Mexico goldmining when their baby was due, so they went to Dallas that the child would by birth be a United States citizen. Later when her husband died, Maude, the daughter of William August Meese (Illinois States Attorney) went to live with her parents in Moline, Illinois.

Brought up in his grandparents' home, his mother teaching, Bill became the special ward of his illustrious grandfather. Owning an island in the Mississippi where they usually spent the summer, much was learned of the lore of Nature in this beautiful area. Bill also pocketed his grandfather's statesmanship and philosophy.

Bill, as he was always called, received his PhD in Chemical Engineering from the University of Iowa in 1934 when he was 26. And Alice Spohn, who he married, received her BM degree from Simpson Conservatory, Indianola, Iowa in 1931 and was taking a summer school course in creative writing at Iowa University when she met Bill.

Being a stranger, she went to the Student Union her first evening and played the beautiful grand piano for a long while.

When she left she was followed, and at the first crossing someone stepped up and said:

"I beg your pardon, but I'm Bill Newton and I just want to tell you how much I enjoyed your playing."

"Thank you!"

"May I walk with you?"

"Yes."

They came to the boarding house where Alice was staying.

"I'm wondering if I could take you out to dinner tomorrow evening?"

Alice hesitated. "You might call me tomorrow."

The next afternoon Alice talked with her motherly landlady and was told:

"I think it would be all right, since he's taking you to dinner."

She was helped with extreme politeness into the front seat of Bill's car, but was horrified to see a bright blanket in the back. She had heard much about university blanket parties. She became stern, offish.

But after having been taken to the city's most elegant TOWN AND GOWN tearoom and enjoyed the first good meal since she'd come, she relaxed. Bill was the most gentlemanly gentleman she'd ever known.

"The bright blanket?" she asked, and with a flourish he spread it out and said it was a keepsake from Mexico, a part of his past.

When summer school was over, she left for Oklahoma to visit her arthritic father whom she adored.

Bill began a profuse letter-writing spree, but with such engineering precision which Alice found rather without sentiment. "Someone else had been found to replace her," she thought pensively.

Bill came for a visit.

Jean (her brother) said, "Bill is like a chicken with its head chopped off. At the show, back to get popcorn, back again for a drink of water."

Returning to Iowa where Alice had been sent as a child to live with her aunt after her mother's death, there came Bill again.

Waiting in her aunt's romantic sunken garden, Alice sat down beside him.

"Alice, if you don't marry me, I'll—Oh, God. I don't want to go through life without you. I've lost everything I ever cared about, mother, everything." Tears were in his eyes.

She leaned over and said, "Then why don't we get married now?"

"You mean it?"

"Yes, more than words can express. So why wait?"

"I don't have a job! This terrible Depression with banks closing and people killing themselves."

"But you will get a job. I have a little teaching money. Let's just get married and strike out."

They were married June 16, 1934 at Osceola, Iowa, in the City Park, standing in front of joined twin oak trees. "Two as one," Alice said.

Soon a job offer came from the Tennessee Valley Authority in Sheffield, Alabama. They began housekeeping in the Sheffield Terrace apartment. Iggie, the cat Alice had picked up at home, was their first pet, both of them ardent animal lovers, they discovered.

Fannie Watson, the aunt, anxious to see for herself how the daughter of her early-dying sister was faring, came for a visit.

While there, President Franklin Roosevelt came. Fannie, a staunch Republican, said: "One can not help but admire him, so crippled and yet so invincible. People starving, his recovery programs have saved the day!"

Months later Bill said, "I do not like this government work. You're taking orders from ignoramuses OR TAKING YOUR LEAVE. What would you say if we quit and went to California?"

"Bill, I'd love to go to California. When shall I start packing?"

He laughed. "You'd head out, not a job in sight?"

"Why not? I'm happy with my writing. Why shouldn't you be happy?"

As the Depression deepened, Bill applied place after place and found to his horror he was "too qualified."

In desperation they took a job going door to door selling a little local newspaper. Hungry, room rent due...

One day Bill got a phone call from a small college in Oregon.

"On the question asking about your religion you left a blank. What church are you affiliated with?"

"None."

"This is a religious college and we do like your qualifications, so if you'll agree to participate in some church activities, the job is yours."

"I am very sorry," Bill said quietly. "I can not honestly do this, as much as I would like the teaching job."

When Bill hung up he said, "I'll starve before I'll be a hypocrite!"

There were tears in his eyes.

Alice, a christian who understood, put her arms around him. "Bill, I love you more for this! We'll starve together."

Before the year was up, Bill had a job in the research division of the Union Oil Company at Redondo Beach.

"See! I told you!"

Before marriage, Alice had bought a Chow puppy she gave to a friend to keep until she now could send for it. Settled, they were ready for a dog. When the frightened ball of fur arrived, she stole their hearts. They called her Teddy for Bill's uncle.

Bill especially liked dogs and said: "This is going to be the extent of our family. The Depression making any job uncertain, food, clothing, schooling."

Shocked at first, Alice decided all she wanted was to write all day long. "*Oh Song of the Prairie Wind!*" It was the story of her parents' early pioneering.

Then Alice's crippled father trundled in, his old Ford fixed up for a place to sleep as well as to cook for himself. He was pleased to help Alice with her book about the past.

Learning of their going hungry, he asked: "Why! Why didn't you write to me for money!"

Surprised, she said, "We never thought of it." Bill agreed, never once did it occur to them to ask someone for money.

One day in 1941, Bill's Engineering Journal arrived and he saw a small ad for a Professor of Chemical Engineering at Georgia Tech. He applied and in a few days received a letter making a tentative offer if he would come for an interview.

"We're off to Georgia!" Alice screamed.

"You utterly amaze me," Bill said.

He got the job. Relaxed, he was now his old happy self.

Settled in, Alice said she would like to rent a piano before she forgot how to play. Bill agreed this was very important because of the songs she kept making up.

"I especially like *Goodbye, Dream Boat.*"

They sang it together.

Goodbye, dream boat
Sailing in the sunset glow
With the only love I'll ever know.
Every moment takes us farther apart.
Soon there'll be the empty sea
Of a lonely heart.

They decided to entertain their new friend, the Viennese composer, and invite their new neighbors they had been enjoying. It was to be the grand occasion of their marriage.

Alas, on the morning of the party Alice woke up with the worst cold she had ever had.

Her call to Bill found him in class. She called her special neighbor, Lucille. Who would want food prepared by her with such a cold!

Lucille spoke of a person who did Christian Science healing and had been known to make ills disappear like magic.

Alice called, was told to read the Bible and sit quietly expecting Christ *who promised to be with us always*, to keep his promise and heal her.

She obeyed, and thought how wonderful it would be if here at last, someone did do what Christ told all to do: "Heal the sick, cleanse the leper." His saying it, meant we could do it! How could anybody call Christ a liar?

She dropped off to sleep.

When she awakened she was healed.

"Lucille! I'm healed! I don't have a cold!"

"I told you!"

The composer came, the dinner was a success, and asked to play her songs after the guest composer finished, she was so elevated she played her best in sheer appreciation.

In the spring of 1945 Bill developed a sinus infection which would not give up; a drier climate needed!

The University of Texas had an opening and he was accepted, so the move began.

"Already I feel better," Bill said, taking a deep breath of the dry air in the land where people were always *wishing* for rain!

"Every leaf is a part of the old dream," he said.

When they reached Austin, Texas, the Chemical Engineering Department gave a party in which the newcomers were introduced, and the teaching start was made.

They liked the old Spanish-style dwelling with its place for pets, and when they went to Bradleys for needed paint, they saw on the high walls many paintings of Texas Bluebonnets and Mexican scenes by Porfirio Salinas. Leaving the store with their paint buckets, Bill stopped and said: "I don't think I can go off and leave that Mexican Scene of the Mission with the waiting horses. It reminds me of my folks living in Mexico several years."

Mr. Bradley was elated. "You may not know it now, but it's a valuable investment. Who knows what it will be worth some day?" The price was four hundred dollars which for them was a lot!

After they left with their picture, Alice said, "It's the bluebonnets I'm dying for."

There was such a difference, teaching at the University.

"Get some outstanding research in the technical journals!" the Dean said.

There was no way Bill could give up being a strong, dependable help to his students for them to learn the subject well enough to make use of it in whatever career was chosen.

"Why did I ever leave Tech?" he kept wondering, his colds now over.

It was only a year later that a letter came from the Dean at Georgia Tech. "Dear Bill: Do we ever need you now! If you really think you're as well as you say, please give us some very serious consideration…

I talked with President Brittain and he's prepared to pay you a thousand dollars more than whatever you're making there."

Alice looked at Bill. He had tears in his eyes.

He said, "If it wouldn't tear up your life, I would like to go."

"A place to write and a place where my Bill is happy is all I want."

"Damn! What'll we do with the farm? I feel like nothing but a yoyo!"

The farm was sold, the bluebonnet painting bought, and since the artist, Porfirio Salinas, lived in San Antonio, they decided to drive down to see him before moving so far away.

They wheeled to San Antonio and came to the small, Spanish-style home of the famed artist and rang the doorbell.

His wife answered and Bill said, "We've bought two of Porfirio's paintings and are moving to Georgia and are hoping to meet the artist before leaving."

The plump Maria said, "I'll see."

Porfirio Salinas came to the door. "How did you get my address?" he asked.

"Mr. Bradley gave it to us," Bill said.

"He isn't supposed to give it to anyone," the husky Mexican said with annoyance.

"Oh, we're sorry!"

Alice said, "Your paintings are so fine! You have the purity of the old masters. We wanted to meet you in person to tell you this."

Porfirio calmed. "Would you like to see what I'm painting now?"

"Yes!" they both replied.

He brought forth a large 42x38 bluebonnet scene, in the center of which was a great leaning tree, rather as if bowing to the bluebonnets.

"We can't go off and leave this painting," Bill stated.

"It isn't finished."

"May we buy it when it is finished?"

"Yes. Selling directly to the buyer, unframed, I'll give it to you for seven hundred dollars."

"I'll give you a check for at least part of it." They could afford, say $300, without going hungry.

Reaching Atlanta, the faculty had a party. "It's about time for the bad penny to return!" said Jess, the Dean. "And you gotta stay with us till you find a place. We already have a fenced-in yard for your pets."

"You'll be sorry!" Bill laughed, pleased.

They found a farm, forty-eight acres. "How much?"

"Thirty-five hundred dollars."

It was but a few days later that Alice received a call from her brother Hugh that their father was near death and asking for her.

She left at once.

Down, down, he had gone.

"Sweet Daddy Mio!" She pressed her cheek against his. "You have to get well enough to come see the place we've bought with its blackberries and sunflowers so we can go blackberrying the way you did as a boy on grandpa's farm!"

She was horrified that he was nothing but a skeleton and came to the place where she could bear no more of this living death.

"Why, God! Why! Please take him!"

It was a week later he seemed to have lost contact with the outside world. But over and over he kept calling her name.

"I'm here, Daddy Mio! I'm here!" Still he called her name. Still she assured him she was here. "Do you want to tell me something, dear heart? I'm right here so tell me!"

When he gulped his last breath she was bitterly relieved.

She turned to stone. How could she believe there was a God of mercy, of Love!

The first thing she said when she returned to Georgia and was met by her tender-hearted Bill was:

"I now understand why you say you're an atheist. I've concluded there can't be a God who would let such a saintly man suffer till every cell in his body is destroyed."

Returning to the old dirty house, Bill said he thought it would give her something else to think about.

Who cared about a house? Who cared about anything!

One morning when she didn't even want to get up, she was half asleep when suddenly she heard a voice. She opened her eyes slightly and saw her mother with her father.

"Here is your father," she said.

He had buckets of paint and said, "We've come to finish your house."

"Daddy Mio!" she called. "Daddy Mio!"

She got up to run and embrace them.

They disappeared.

The incident was so real that she immediately found assurance that her loved parents were in the eternity of God's Love.

Soon the rural mail carrier brought a letter in which was the settlement of her father's estate including an inheritance check.

"Oh, Daddy Mio," she wept over such a father, living in his car to have plenty to leave his children.

Their old poorly built house could be made into something decent after all. "Please, God, tell my father how much the check will help!"

"Bill!" she ran to meet him when he drove up.

They put in a bathroom, hired carpenters, built a study for Bill with a fireplace, his own shower and clothes closet.

Porfirio's old Mission went over the fireplace, while the bluebonnets with their big tree had its place in the front room with its unpainted oak walls. She made drapes of matching blue.

"There is just one thing missing," she said.

"What's that?"

"In the front room I don't like the cheap print on the south wall."

Bill laughed. "I know. Another Bluebonnet picture."

"It would be nice to have a red barn—insignificantly placed in the background—as a match for the red leather furniture."

"Sounds right to me. Get it as your reward for pulling us out of the worst mess I've ever been in."

Three months later when the picture tube arrived, Alice was afraid to open it. What could she do with a big red barn with a few bluebonnets? Slowly she twisted off the top and drew out the tube. She spread the picture before her.

She burst into tears.

It was so beautiful she could do nothing but sit there and weep.

"Oh, Porfirio! How could I ever have doubted that Master touch!"

In the spring Bill bought a garden tractor and plowed up an acre of the land back of the house and had stable manure hauled till it was three inches thick.

"Anybody putting on that much manure don't know what he's doing," neighbors said.

But the months brought the firm belief that Bill Newton's garden was the best to be found. Such flavor in the tomatoes, cucumbers, corn, etc.

The worn-out Georgia soil had lost its flavoring elements it seemed.

He showered the Georgia Tech faculty and neighbors with produce until some of the faculty turned their thoughts to moving to the country.

Dr. Elmer Rhodes and wife, from the Physics Department, did move a mile down the road from the Newtons. Before the move he asked Bill: "What is your criteria for buying a farm?"

"Just one. Without any personal facilities inside or out, it is necessary to have plenty of trees and bushes."

The gentleman that he was, never having in all his life lived without a bathroom, made it even funnier. Their Bill was a real helluva engineer at Georgia Tech with its Rambling Wrecks!

They bought a chow dog named Loupe and bred her with their male dog, Amigo, and Loupe came forth with four tumbling, rolling balls of fur.

Clementine, Nickey, Caramba, and Montezuma. It was indeed the family complete, a farm with stock, even their two riding horses they enjoyed on their rides through the clearings.

Bill decided they must have a furnace since there also would be dogs to keep warm on cold winter nights. Fireplaces just didn't do the job. He hired Tech students who were always needing extra money.

It was decided that husky Norman Briggs should crawl under the house to be sure the fuel pipes were well secured. Ready to go back to Atlanta, Norman Briggs said:

"Doc, what is this on my neck? It just stung me."

"Black widow!"

Bill began to slit the bite and use a suction cup, and being such a thorough person, he didn't stop till he was sure.

They drove him to the hospital where his wife Kathy was on duty as a nurse.

She fainted.

The doctor examined the incision, made tests, and said: "Your professor couldn't have done better. He saved your life. Lucky you."

The big fellow laughed and said, "Doc's my luck. I have a lotta livin' to do yet!"

"Don't we all!" Bill said, feeling the ruin of his life if he had been the cause of his student's death.

One evening after Alice had prepared two delectable what the butcher called "hand-painted T-bone steaks" she was shocked to hear Bill say,

"Please don't fix me any more meat."

"Why!"

"I can't bear for an animal to be killed just to appease my appetite."

Alice said softly, "Okay." She was afraid she was going to cry. "I'm sorry! The dogs will enjoy it."

Why could she go on eating meat? Why! Why!

Because, she concluded as the weeks wore on, she didn't see food, hamburgers and drumsticks, as something once alive anymore than sweet corn, the wheat in the bread. In Bill's beautiful garden the plants flourished under his loving care. She hoped they didn't mind being eaten.

She carried his huge, perfect cabbage to the State Fair. All the way by bus she was most protective that not a leaf be damaged.

"Don't forget the cabbage!" she reminded the bus driver at every stop.

"How could I!" he shouted loudly, to the amusement of all. The cabbage was the last to come out.

"Wow!" someone said. "That's a cabbage that am a cabbage. Did you grow it?"

"My husband did."

"Can I have a nibble?"

"No!" everyone shouted.

The cabbage did take BEST IN THE SHOW, so the ribbon to take home to Bill pleased him. "Worth my wearisome work."

To further his own learning, Bill decided to go to MIT for a two-week crash course in math. When the class concluded each was given a diploma. Bill accepted his by saying, "I consider this a diploma for having successfully crossed Massachusetts Avenue every morning without getting killed."

"How true!" they laughed.

Now and then Bill brought home Georgia Tech's foreign students to give them a little encouragement and country relaxation. It was a treat for all. They especially liked Suresh Candra and his wife Shakuntaia from India. Pooman, their big-eyed amber child was soon called Pumpkin because of her funful ways. Mulkul, their small son, was a whirl of mischief.

One day Bill asked, "How's your writing coming?"

"I write some every day. It's my tranquilizer."

The letter of acceptance was received, on her manuscript titled The Reminiscing Wind and when the first copy arrived, Alice found all in order and even the pictures turned out clearly.

Bill was pleased and said it had been many years of dedicated work, coming up with something of real value.

Finally the year of retirement came. Bill was more than ready. He was tired, nothing more pleasant than lots of sleep.

Suddenly Alice was awakened in the night by strange moaning. She found him unconscious and grabbed the phone to call the Rhodes.

"Bill's bad sick! Call the ambulance while I get dressed!"

The Rhodes came with pajamas, slippers, and shaving needs.

When they reached the hospital, the driver wheeled Bill in while Alice rushed forth in search of a doctor and to call her faithful Christian Science practitioner for herself.

Dr. Mims asked if Bill had ever before had such a siege.

"Never."

Two weeks later he did go home. Once in a while he complained about not being able to think clearly, was told he'd "lost his *electrolites*."

They thought about trading their farm for some wheat land in Oklahoma. Bill asked Alice to go look. "Find a big wheat farm and look for something with a big red barn."

The first thing Alice was shown was a big wheat farm with a big red barn and a large quonset hut where machinery was stored. There were huge trees, a large frame house with running water including two bathrooms; a big rolling pasture along with the wheat land, three hundred and twenty acres in all. Alice called Bill.

"I've found it! All you want and more!"

"Tell them we'll take it before they change their minds!"

"I already have!"

Bill died suddenly early in March, the move to have been made in May.

It was three years later that Alice built a house on old Spohn farm west of Beaver, Oklahoma. Here she still resides, moving on and on in her ship of timeless faith. A life overflowing as theirs had been was like a mighty river...where could it end!

CHAPTER 9

PATHS OF WONDERING
(Published by The Golden Quill Press, 1975)

There are trailing paths of wondering
Through which to sort one's ticklish way,
Like: does a tree believe in God?
This seraphic lily, does it pray?

I wonder, wonder, wonder...
Which bird composed its brother's song,
Or how a spruce can grow symmetrically,
Not a single branch too long.

SONGS BY THINGS

I hear soft, immortal music
In the wind as it bends the trees
Like a child at random play
With only itself to please.

I hear sweet, soft strains when people
Who think not a thing of their cost
Forfeit days of urgent need
To search for a child some far-where lost.

I hear soft, immortal music
In the rain, the storms, green trumpets of Spring;
In the barks, the silence, the sobs,
And I stop, I stop and ask a meadow to sing.

I AGREE WITH GOD

Unknowingly people say a dog's a dog.
But I agree with God.
As mine looks up with only the want
To be allowed to stay,

I see her love so there it makes me ask,
Who am I to be endowed with such affection?
Am I her own invented god
To trust, believe, and worship?

When people say a dog is just a dog
I often think,
What kind of thing does that
Make tawdry, impatient me?

And then with God, I must agree.
A dog is a bit of flesh and bones and plume
With a little touch of extra.
However mean or poor his people are,

He loves and loves and loves
And what he puts into words
With an incessantly talkative tail
Leaves human language flat.

THE FENCE AROUND THE CORN

The lowly posts around the corn
Have been righteous citizens for years.
Doing not what they thought they would
When they towered over yonder glades.

Dreams collapsed with a violent crash
As they were hacked to make a post.
But no louder than a mother's trauma
When Death appears with its trumpet.

It comforts the shattering heart to note
That a tree provides a fence post.
And a wobbling new-born calf
Is safe with a mother fenced from corn.

The fallen tree has regained its place
Its dignity, and a kind of heaven-penciled grace.

AS A PILOT IN TROUBLE

(Written in 1964)

I long to see all the world at prayer.
Every nation and hamlet and far-country there.
If together just once, we all stopped and prayed,
Mayhap the concorde'd bare the span the Creator made
When He called the earth good, behold, very good.

How I yearn to see all the world at prayer,
Every young one, and cripple, and ruffian there,
Not a human left out in this hour to pray
As a pilot in trouble would pray.
I wonder, Oh, I wonder, what'd come, such a day!

CHAPTER 10

A TOUR OF THE BLOSSOMING PRAIRIE
(Published by The Standard Printing Company, Amarillo, TX, 1994)

We can tell by the beauty of nature that God adores us! So many wildflowers, fragrant grasses, trees, mountains, lakes, along with the great oceans with their feathery white caps, all not only planted but arranged with artistry and affection!

I am very fond of sunflowers. In fact, they're my favorites. They are so cheerful with their bright yellow petals and dark centers. They wave and smile in the breeze and they line my country road to town as though our Creator knew well that I couldn't help but feel loved and cheered as I went about my business.

I even have these sunflower beauties looking in my windows, growing where no man ever thought of planting these great tall stalks that endure heat and storms un-scathed year after year, like special companions that know they are as loved as I am.

Add your favorites to the list of these special gestures of the divine's caring.

Maybe we've lost everything in a fire, earthquake, or tornado.

When we see the grandness of the earth with all its glories totally un-manmade, we know very well a God that loving does not send things to destroy us.

Would Christ have been able to still a raging sea about to destroy God's disciples, if the storm were God sent?

"My thoughts are not your thoughts, and neither are your ways My ways," He tells us. "As the heavens are higher than the earth, so are My thoughts higher than your thoughts." (*Isa. 55:9*)

Man made in God's likeness with Christ the one eternal pattern, we need human logic which has to conclude totally with a God of peace, beauty, and immutable harmony... all else man's heeding the Serpent that egged man into being a god on his own.

Oh, how man does plod along by himself!

We need to keep as made and directed as the wildflowers.

At least these beautiful suddenly-appearing glories do present a challenge!

I'm ashamed at least not to try to be as flawless as a petunia.

The divine Parent who created these many different flowers for our pleasure created us! Are these blooms little reminders that we in His likeness are meant to be flawless? Not sandburs; a pleasing bloom but awfully stickery?

One of us succeeded: the Christ, a man pattern we crucified.

Living in the country in beautiful Windmill Valley, even in my 89th year, I find unfailing strength in my garden of un-man-planted blooms, patterns to live by as well as promises of our Creator ever near.

The real joy is being a part of it all! With all our divine gifts, how can we help but feel loved?

CHAPTER 11

LIVE KNOWING YOU HAVE FOREVER
(Published by Marshall Jones Company, 1993)

We have been promised life is eternal, so why not live knowing we have forever? Being old myself, I find death holds no dread for me. Death sings of a better tomorrow and I'm ready to go any time and do hope I have done less harm than good over these 89 years, as eternity is a long time for regretting.

Throughout all eternity we have the Christ Pattern free of mortal ills and old age to turn to. What more do we need to be assured life is eternal than this Christ example?

As soon as our earth bound bodies are shed, the true spiritual (Christly) self ascends above this very trying but teaching earth school. Even the worst criminal (all life impossible to be anything but God created) has a spiritual self buried though it is in hates and crime. Christ proved this telling such to "go and sin no more." Even his crucifiers.

The real Spirit-likeness self is the forever self that is never destroyed, as Christ proved raising the dead. It is very comforting to be a part of infinity's vast forever.

We should indeed begin today to live knowing we have forever!

No push. No hurry.

We're God's Spirit's, likeness spiritual which keeps us as far above the Serpent's lies of mortal belief as the morning star! Man is a phenomenon. So much to puzzle over. Doesn't it make you want to start learning at least some of the answers to life's wonderments?

We need to learn puzzling facts that come to mind, like is every star inhabited in some way? There is something divine above that beautiful canopy of stars, a sort of crowning glory to all the beauties of earth! Sunsets, sunrises, tall pines, lilies floating on lakes, snow capped mountains. It speaks of the Creator as a lover of the beautiful.

"Why is there sometimes a freeze that kills spring's start?"

This, we don't know. But God does.

Life here is a school. There are endless lessons to be learned! Sometimes man needs disciplining. One year after a beautiful winter came a killing snowstorm where all man could do was to stay inside and try every way possible to keep warm.

Was God destroying marihuana-growing plants? Was He making His adored children seek warmth and shelter rather than scatter about dope-taking with abandon?

God of purer eyes than to behold iniquity is not unknowing of His Kingdom. Storms where man kneels in prayer to be saved are hard lessons in the earth school.

What can always be remembered is that God, Spirit, creates nothing but the spiritual. It's what He sees.

We do not have every knowable fact. I am writing on the waves of intuition…In praying and listening for the truth, I write what I hear deep down.

Christ said he could of himself do nothing. "As I hear, I judge."

Just knowing this is what Christ does helps. We are very adored by our Creator. Even a blooming peach tree, a purple violet, a wild rose, proves it.

Back at the beginning that old Serpent coiled around the Tree of Good and Evil tempted Eve and Adam to be gods themselves rather than to bow to some God Who required them to be in His likeness. Even many of us who do our best know always it falls short of any God created best. God finally sent Christ Jesus to prove what this spiritual likeness to Spirit is.

With life eternal we may through the eons of time find ourselves in one school after another. We do have to be the likeness of God, all eternity though it take, Christ our one example. Crucifying our one person sent to demonstrate the real spiritual likeness of God, is man's unredeemable sin. But God is Love this shows still God cares! So onward is the only direction for us to go.

No wonder we have been given forever!

One night I had a dream that I myself had died. At the funeral, all prettied up in a pretty casket, I remember that when the singing and un-bothered-about mumbles were over, I sat up and said:

"I thank you for your kind attention!"

Being a child, my mother having recently died, the event had not been too impressive, the dream would indicate.

Death should be earth-life graduation with the hope that we graduate with honors.

This is of course not to make light of death. When we lose a loved one we are torn into a thousand shreds! My husband whom I had adored and couldn't bear life without, died suddenly. Never can we get over the death of someone for whom we care deeply!

It is our own death I speak of as nothing to dread, life is forever! ...Who knows what all lies ahead, with plenty of time to learn all there is to learn! Our inborn zest to learn helps us get ready for what comes next.

Heaven is the home of the spiritual. Never forget this! Christ Jesus said the kingdom of heaven is at hand. So the real spiritually eternal self was what he saw when he said it...Think of the times he proved it. Never did he fail to prove it (healing thousands, seeing the spiritual self as the real, only self). You are spiritual when you care, are sorry for the sick, the hungry, and the forgotten who revert to crime as their only means of survival. You are spiritual when you get to the point where you have to say, God help me! Help me! No other direction to turn. You are spiritual when you suddenly find you're relieved that life is eternal and you do have forever to be that person you honestly wish you were.

God all Love, who knows what He has to prove that Love is never ending?

Love loves us too much to give up. Thank goodness!

CHAPTER 12

THE HANDLE OF THE PAN
(Published by The Herald Democrat, Beaver, OK)

Few lands have been owned consecutively by five nations, although never fought over for possession, as was the now Panhandle of Oklahoma, prehistorically possessed by wandering tribes of American Indians.

There were good reasons why this 168-mile long, 34-mile wide strip of land extending west from Oklahoma, south of Kansas and north of Texas as it nosed into New Mexico, was not wanted permanently by Spain, France, England, Mexico, nor the United States of America. The strip was mostly flat, nothing to stop the blizzards in winter nor the scorching winds of summer. All that grew on these plains were buffalo grass, sagebrush, and soapweeds. There were wandering Indians with their bows and arrows, coyotes, rattlesnakes, badgers, skunks, some lobo wolves, and now and then bear and antelope in the river areas.

The United States issued permission for citizens to file on claims in the free land, and the town of Beaver City finally emerged. In 1887 an election was held in which the citizens divided the Strip into three counties, first Beaver County, next Texas County, and lastly Cimarron County. The town of Guymon was becoming a popular point. In fact, in 1890 Guymon was named the Capitol City of the Oklahoma Panhandle, with fast growing stores, schools, churches, and an established local government with laws and officials to enforce the laws.

Beaver City came up with the first newspaper, The Territorial Advocate, published by E. E. Eldridge and Mr. Estes, in 1887. Like Guymon, the towns were becoming organized by adventurous, well-educated people of the nation who were enticed by the offer of 160 acres of free land.

The chief interest in Guymon was the rapid growth of a school to promote agricultural practices. It was named The Panhandle Agricultural Institute in 1909. Today, in 1995, it has an enrollment of 2,000.

One of the most beautiful scenes of the nation is the sandhills north of Beaver. The sand of the hills is as fine as table salt, and its hue is a salmon pink. The total bareness was spoiled during the dust-storm years when the hills were covered with top soil which grew vegetation in the lower edges. The area has been made a State Park with camping facilities.

There are also the colorful red clay banks of Home Creek which make snaky winds west of Beaver where cottonwood trees give beauty to the Panhandle's flatness. They bear the courage and strength of the early pioneers. One great old tree is believed to be 120 years old, a landmark where horsemen tied their teams while shopping in Beaver.

In the Spring, the area is a colorful garden of wildflowers, cacti, and soapweeds (yucca) that boast stalks of white bells. Other flowers are Indian daisies (galardia), prairie gold, sunflowers, and pincushion cacti with pink blooms, mitten cacti with large yellow blooms, morning-glory bushes that appear as baskets of pink trumpets, goldenrod, queen-anne's lace, horse mint, poke weed, tall thistles with purple "shaving-brush" blooms, and of course forever the tumbleweeds that break loose in the fall and frighten teams as they come tumbling in the wind.

Another familiar sight on the prairies of the Panhandle is the faithful, ever-needed windmill. With the continuous wind, water for the farmers with their cattle, sheep, and horses is always available.

The song of the windmill brings peace, an old tin cup hanging within easy reach, you sip and say, "Ummm good."

Every Spring Beaver hosts a cowchip throwing contest in which the person who tosses the dried cattle dung the farthest gets a trophy.

The lowly cow-and-buffalo chips were the only means of heat for warmth and cooking food back at the beginning when people came to the prairie and filed on claims. No coal, no trees for wood. The contest came forth from the old days moving along over the prairie stopping here and there to toss the dried dung into the wagon, often seeing who could toss from the greatest distance.

The yearly contest began in 1969 when a group of Beaver people were anxious to come up with an idea for attracting visitors. Why not something to honor the brave ones who hung on midst every hardship imaginable? The event was such a success that every year from then on, the cowchip throw has been the main event. Now Beaver is named THE COWCHIP CAPITAL OF THE WORLD, an honor we enjoy, knowing the value of the chip to the early settlers.

Oklahoma's Panhandle is very productive in its farming industry. Being flat land, this gives the farmer not only the native buffalo grass for cattle grazing, but good fertile fields for wheat which is the principle crop. After the wheat is cut the land is free for planting kafircorn, maise, broomcorn and of course sweetcorn for food. Also hay, alfalfa, millet, and cane for sorgum are grown.

The discovery of oil in which the land is dotted with the slow pumping wells, has given the Strip an important boost. Towns have hospitals, fine schools, handsome homes, nursing homes for those old pioneers, impressive courthouses, and museums to house the early keepsakes including the buggies and wagons which were the only way to travel the long dusty trails.

The town even has its famous. Ross Rizley became a part of the state legislature, was assistant Secretary of Agriculture, and became a federal judge appointed by President Eisenhower. Maude Thomas came to Beaver from Missouri in 1886. She was one of the first newspaper editors, refused liquor ads, was chairman of the Red Cross, established Beaver's First Christian Church, was head of Pen Women, Eastern Star, and won a national award for instigating the Heritage Trail.

Tim Leonard in his climb in the state is an active senator. Dr. Ed Calhood is State President of the National Heritage Society.

To me, all citizens are important with their friendliness, courage, patience, vision. It's a town where every citizen is your special friend, I have found!

CHAPTER 13

WHAT HAPPENED TO GOD'S VERY GOOD?
(Published by Marshall Jones Company, 1989)

> FORSAKE THOSE THAT LOVE THEE,
> BUT NEVER THE RIGHT.
> —ANONYMOUS

OH, WHAT HAS HAPPENED TO GOD'S *VERY GOOD?*

We need to know. We have the right to know. To begin, maybe you have experienced the reality of Christ's promise to be with us always, bearing that very good, and will delight to know how others have. So share now with me some actual proofs that we're not just looking for some fantasy.

People who honestly do not believe in some God, such as my husband whose Christly qualities included cutting out meat "so an animal won't have to be killed just to appease my appetite," are deep reasoners who may pray to some Something, they don't know what, but can not "intelligently" believe in some far-off God that made everything and called it very good. "Just look about you!"

As a small child, I not only felt a definite nearness to Christ Jesus but am convinced he was responsible for my overcoming typhoid fever from which the doctor said I could not possibly survive (1911). Finally moving on into my teens I turned away from religion, pouring all my energies into becoming the musician my early-deceased mother was... On with that career until writing sent me to the University of Iowa where I met my future mate who was as near an atheist as I've ever known.

It was not until after we married, had weathered Depression hunger and finally emerging from that into the brilliance of his teaching at Georgia Tech, that my love for Christ returned. We invited our neighborhood to enjoy a dinner concert in our home featuring a Viennese composer my husband had met. Struck on the day with a violent cold, my neighbor said I should call a "divine healer" which I did and the cold disappeared.

I discovered there are many who believe Christ meant it when he said that we should heal the sick, cleanse the leper. In fact, my healer was a follower of Mary Baker Eddy who founded an entirely new religion based on the assurance that we could do as Christ said, very positive he wouldn't have said it if it weren't possible. We are told "God is a Spirit, and they that worship him must worship him in Spirit and in truth." (John 4:24)

If God is "a Spirit" and creates everything spiritual (*His likeness*) could it be that WE OURSELVES are seeing wrong? Christ Jesus told us:

"Having eyes, see ye not?" (*Mark 4:18*)

"And he said unto them, he that hath ears to hear, let him hear." *(Mark 4:9)*

I've listened. Our Creator Spirit, His likeness can't be anything but spiritual.

We concede that the field of science with its endless research has brought priceless gains in numberless ways: flown to the moon, explored the stars, found ways to ease pain, replace organs, enhance hearing and seeing.

Of a solid direction in search of the good we seek, does it not nudge us to look deeper into the truth the Galilean promised would free us of life's tribulations?

Christ Jesus taught that God is a Spirit who creates spiritually which is and all *mental process*.

When the spiritual is added to our wavering material theories we find life changing for better or worse in proportion to man's reliance on this Spirit influence—as opposed to material chance, natural selection.

SPIRIT. WHAT IS SPIRIT YOU CALL GOD, ITS LIKENESS SPIRITUAL?

Think of people dear to you who are deceased. The qualities remaining are their love, loyalty, patience, etc., all undecaying qualities that hold our devotion.

This is spiritual perceiving, above the material. In the laboratory the splitting of the atom has broken this once thought the minutest of particles down into "a point of spinning nothingness traveling at the velocity of light," clear to the religious that thought could be a powerful influence on such *unsolid substance* appearing solid.

The field of material science is not to be unconditionally accepted until the powerful Spirit-force Christ made use of is fully incorporated...We're looking for the *very good* Christ discovered, proved, and lived. Scientific discoveries which reduce matter to "spinning nothingness" have a real bearing on what the Galilean prophet disclosed.

When we leave out the divine immensity of our Creator, Spirit filling the whole space, we find our little world full of hate, sickness, trials, wars, and beliefs that we are entirely on our own. Can we find a more clear, understandable origin of species which the God Creator called *very good* than Christ Jesus who came to teach us to do as he-and more?

He said for us to "Love thy Lord with all thy heart, soul and mind. *(Matt. 2:2)*

IS THIS SOMETHING WE CAN'T MANAGE?

The Holy Bible is the writings of those who have glimpsed truths through Time and wanted to share them.

With the first chaper we learn freeing truths. God (*Spirit*) and man in His likeness (spiritual).

Perhaps religionists themselves believe Adam spoiled it for us when succumbing to the serpent's enticement to become gods. Adam to blame for today's wilderness of disease and distress! Christ's command: "Be ye perfect, even as your Father which is in heaven is perfect" (*Matt. 5:48*) has a request which forces us back to man before Adam (*God's likeness*).

Christ certainly exemplifies the undefeatable Law that brought even himself from the tomb.

Impossible for us since the Christ was sent as God's "Only Son"? Why then did Jesus say with such insistence that we should do as he and more?

DOESN'T THAT HAVE TO MEAN WE CAN?

What hidden potential are we leaving out in this humdrum, trial-ridden existence?

IS THERE TRULY A *VERY GOOD* IN OUR MIDST?

Darwin said: "As natural selection works solely by and for the good of each being, all corporeal and mental endowments will tend to progress toward perfection." (*Origin of Species*) Agnostics brush aside religion with total honesty. But it does not brush away God.

So let us seek facts which are receptacles that hold answers. Something is missing on the material trail, and who knows but it's the very thing we're looking for?

Our Galilean said, "I can of myself do nothing." (*John 5:30*) The freest thing in the world is our ability to reason through to facts that can't be refuted. Why not to the truth that Christ promised would free us as it freed the lepers, stilled the seas? Adam lost the beginning peace. How? Why? Can it ever be regained? Suppose we let what keeps the heart going be the source of an intelligence so beyond us that we in our years of doubts and questions can afford to attribute *more* to this astounding heart-beat source. Is it the evolutionary urge to strive on and on till we iron out every despairing wrinkle and get to a finished species? If there is a better way, how can we capture a little of the calm we glimpse in God's man *In The Beginning* who seemed to possess the perfection Christ expects of us?

The average American's ideal is to pile his car full with tent, sleeping bags, fishing rods, a skillet, and a bucket for making coffee over an open fire. He collects road maps and goes to the mountains where he can pitch camp in the most uninhabited place he can find. "Oh, God, what peace."

We are so used to accepting what the majority accepts that we honestly do not know what is buried down inside our own marvelous reasoning without limit.

It is out *spiritual spark* that overcomes despairs, even fears. The three Hebrew men, Shadrach, Abednego, and Meshach allowed themselves to be thrown into the fiery furnace to prove God is real. (*Dan 1:7*) When the spiritual sense is allowed to grow to its fullest extent, we are able to find a oneness with Spirit Who brings peace, answers.

God is LOVE, the Bible tells us, and this Love (when allowed) comes flowing through our lives with such a wave of peace and unfretful living, it does find practicality for the troubled heart. The world is full of wonders, we ourselves the biggest of our aweing wonders. But to overcome our persistent cloud of unexplainable discontents, one drinks, swears, bets, smokes, wanders about for anything that appeases. How could there be a God when the world is full of little but sick, sorrowing people warring, hating, killing; while at the same time wanting only to find some sort of contentment? Either we have lost our way, or there is no way.

What if we had faith in nothing but the Law that healed Lazarus?

Christ got away with it saying: "I can of myself do nothing." The "material" body being to him created by his Father Spirit, thus spiritual, changed from its discords to the harmony and influence of Spirit.

Here again the materially minded scientist as well as the spiritually-minded believer can glimpse the unsolid of the solid, a whole new field where infinite Laws and intelligence meet. Man's slavery not only looms self-imposed on this God-created road, but it could be that man alone can wipe out his incompletions. We long to be Christlike but science would have our evolutionizing selves a million years from that state.

But we all possess the means to be decent. Children especially, and they are the future. What are we handing them? Our mistakes, shortcomings? Or truths that free?

If that which "tells" the child when to stop growing teeth, measures the length of each eyelash, were trusted completely to guide that fresh budding "good" would it? Our part, prayer for help, guidance? What keeps the earth turning and fills a tree with luscious pears made us.

We are amazing creatures who can invent airplanes that fly faster than the speed of sound.

Yet bigger penitentiaries, higher walls, tougher guards are still our only answers to a safe, aspiring community. The Bible is full of prophets who had more than unshakable faith to stand on. Today man even doubts there is a God. Why should we doubt that that which maintains us is not powerful enough to guide and save us? To clean oneself out of all mortal fears and destructive beliefs, to be nothing but the cousin to a tiny blue ageratum, to long to be all we were created to be, and to keep infinitely grateful for the ability to think—is a start! Both God's original *very good* man and the Christ are our two human examples of perfection.

Instead of trying to find a missing link in some buried ruins, we may find it our spirituality which links us to Spirit (God) where we are as free as the first man, a dominion that gives us full rule over our serpents no matter how loudly they try to tell us it's no use, it's all a fairy tale, life is too hard to do anything but scramble to keep well and keep food on the table.

Christ fed thousands, stilled storms, uncovering life's full potential.

God Spirit, we His likeness, are we not impelled to keep spiritual to experience

God's very good which Christ was sent to demonstrate and did to such pure perfection?

Reason says *nothing at all* has happened to God's very good, to that real spiritual, eternal you which you find trying hard to do what's right.

It's the trying that keeps you spiritual!

Remember what we learned in grade school? "If at first you don't succeed, try, try again."

CHAPTER 14

ON THE WINGS OF TOMORROW
(Published by The Golden Quill Press, 1984)

After soaring o'er life's terrain of years,
Plus three score ten, at today's Tetons climbed,
I have found to my comforting favor
Tomorrow is better. I have learned from today.

Who can sorrow o'er his ripening age
When every tomorrow bears the hopper
Of fruit from the lofty ledge of this day?
Green the plums now, but how quickly they ripen

By dire need to sweeten acrid regrets.
O the urge to pray more for grace to grow
In understanding of self, of God, and friends
Who betrayed, forgot, or blindly hurt.

Every devastating storm I have braved,
Every defeat that has shattered my heart
Has in slow and painful overcoming
Found with morning, a gift of furbished strength.

HOUR OF NEED

Years of The Depression, hour of need.
Devastated lands and distraught people,
Dust-black noons of food-growing soil;
A whole Nation deep in the dark of want.

"We can not marry. We can not marry!"
"We can make it together I know, I know!"
"Whatever comes I want to be with you."
"I must search alone or I'll die of fear!"

"With each other to keep us from falling,
Oh, I will not let you go on alone.
Say Yes! Say Yes! It's the only way love
Will have it. You can not trudge along alone!"

Laughter cracking the spell of the panic.
"Whoever thought I would be proposed to?
Girls can say No. But what does a man say?
Tables turned—guess I'd crash if you refused!"

LEAVING THE NEST

The jalopy that had served on campus
Carried the newlyweds far to the West
To rent a rundown cottage (ten dollars).
Then off took Bill to hunt for an anchor.

In the window sat a bowl of peanuts.
"I have 'leven cents; we can buy them.
Ready shelled they should stretch a day or two."
O peanuts, freshly roasted, sweet heaven!

An ad for a couple, door to door search
For new subscribers to small, local news
Moved them swiftly to grasp their final straw.
Rent due, what food? Even sold their best clothes.

On the morrow they knocked with soaring hopes.
Scar-streaked doors, sagging doors, fancy doors.
Evening returning they had no order.
Holding back tears kept words barely spoken.

"Now, you gotta insist till they give in.
Insist!" said Boss. "Just don't ever give in.
Show them our sports, recipes. They'll give in.
You can do it. I hired you knowing so."

Ah, tomorrow they changed, come sweet morning
A woman said Yes and gave them a dollar,
Another slammed the door in cold contempt,
A man gave them a five for year's promise.

The years of learning to be an engineer,
"What a waste. And it's even against me,
Damned credentials. I don't fit anywhere!
A whole life wasted. Only a peddler."

*It was late. They drove on and looked for gas.
Fifteen cents, eighten cents, then fourteen cents.
"It'll have to be twelve to get me to work'n back."
"Why is it so high here? Red sells for twelve."*

*"Red's special. He's been penniless, too.
Knows what it's like hunting or getting to work."
"I see thirteen cents up ahead. Could you
Get what we can and then—hold our breath?"*

THE ANSWER

*"Why did you pick this day to go to town?
An exam to get ready, a lecture!
After this if you're not ready I'll leave.
Oh, for catsake!" He stopped. Began to back.*

*"What are you backing for! Are you crazy?"
"Little turtle in the road. Can't leave him there!"
At last he stopped, got out, gently picked it up and
Carried it far from the busy highway.*

*"I'm sorry, my delay!" Bess said in tears.
"Now I know why I love you. Now I know!"
She sobbed. "Once or twice I've wondered. Sky fall!
Above all else...a wee, helpless turtle."*

CHAPTER 15

CHRIST AS A CLOSE COMPANION;
(Published by Marshall Jones Company, 1991)

We have been told from youth that God created the universe including the earth upon which he sent man to inhabit with all the wealth, beauty and necessities furnished for joyous living. But centuries later He found that man with his gift of free will had made a mess of things. So He sent His Son to show man what was created in abundance for a life of glorious living. But we hung this divine way-shower on a cross calling him a liar. So God re-called him. But not before this rescuer of mankind said he would be their stay always.

In England two women claimed to have heard messages from the "Living Christ himself," recorded in a book titled *God Calling*, published by Dodd Mead & Co.

His message for June 1 reads:

"Not so much the asking me to make you this or that but the living with Me, thinking of Me, talking to Me—thus you grow like me...Love me. Rest in Me. Joy in me."

The one that inspired the writing of my own companionship came on February 29. "How little man knows and senses My need of Love and Companionship."

Since childhood I have loved Christ Jesus. As far as I was concerned, this was as true as the love of my own parents.

To have Christ as a close companion is to know a life far above sordid, unsatisfying mortality. There's a song:

> *"I walk with Love along the way,*
> *And O, it is a holy day:*
> *No more I suffer cruel fear,*
> *I feel God's presence with me here:*
> *The joy that none can take away is mine;*
> *I walk with Love today."*
> (From Christian Science Hymnal, page 427)

In our Companioning with this resurrected Christ, we realize he tried very hard to teach us what is true, what God is and what we are in His likeness.

"Pray for more faith, as a thirsty man in a desert prays for rain, for water. Swift comes My help, swift and strong. Do you know what it is to feel sure that I can never fail you? ... How poor is man's faith!" (*God Calling, p. 51*)

Over the years we do find that life with Christ Jesus is a Love story truer than one can imagine. Even if he hadn't promised himself available in which we can not make too many demands, the constant, ever-present love, the pure, divine caring would be enough to make any effort to "acquaint oneself with the Lord and be at peace."

How can we hate our fellowman when we know Christ Jesus is loving all as a father loves his family, including the wayward as demonstrated in the story of the Prodigal Son? When the son caught a glimpse of his father running to him, he surely grew more fearful. But weak and desolate, he knew whatever came he had to take it.

Imagine the shock when his father fell upon him and kissed him in a burst of love and relief.

Isn't this bound to be a favorite with all Bible students?

We have to claim our heritage as sons and daughters of the divine

Maybe you are saying: "Oh, how I wish I had the faith you have."

Where does faith come from?

What gift could Love bestow on us of more value than Faith?

If we pray for faith—more faith—can we not have the faith that Love will supply all we need and more?

"He that cometh to God must believe that he is a rewarder of them that diligently seek him. Never doubt. Have no fear. Watch the faintest tremor of fear, and stop all work, everything, and rest before Me until you are joyful and strong again." (*God Calling*, May 9)

These words of the Christ come like a refreshing rain on a parched field, when we become close companions with the Christ. And the more we cultivate our mustard seed of faith the more our companioning with Christ Jesus grows. To "walk with Love along the way," as the song goes, is to know God has made us divine entities superior to any mortal idea we may have of ourselves.

It was "Through spiritual ascendency your Lord and Master healed the sick, raised the dead, and commanded even the winds and waves to obey him." (*Science & Health* by Mary Baker Eddy, p.67)

This spiritual consciousness is the first need, not only in our Christ companioning but in our understanding as we follow him. . . "Seeking is not sufficient. It's our striving that opens doors." (*Science & Health*, p. 341)

One of our biggest evils is fear. How many times a day do we not fear little things if not big ones?

Good is one of Christ's names for God. What to fear in good? We are talking about the exact opposite of evil.

As for me, I accept Christ's definition that God is the only good. It makes an unvarying basis, like the multiplication table.

When fear attacks, we can know the good that is God is never absent and His power is unopposable.

"To hold yourself superior to sin, because God made you superior to it and governs man, is true wisdom... To hold yourself superior to sickness and death is equally wise. To fear them is impossible, when you fully apprehend God and know that they are no part of His creation." (*Science & Health*, p. 211:20)

This from *God Calling* (Sept. 11) "You do not make yourselves loving and strong and patient and humble. You live with Me, and then My Life accomplishes the miracle change."

It would seem that the divine Creator, all Love, loves His creation regardless of any love returned.

The greatest gift from God is our *freedom*. We can serve God, or iron-ruling mortality.

For me, I'll stand with the loving Christ who says, "When the soul finds its home of rest in Me, then it is that real life begins." (*Misc.*, p. 5)

CHAPTER 16

MY SONG OF MANY LOVES
(Published by The Golden Quill Press, 1985)

THESE MANY LOVES

Ah, so many loves, no end, no end!
The cool, day-break hours of Summer
When all the birds rejoice in chorus,
Try each others' trees, explore the sky.
Can we be sad while the bobolinks
Glory in their lilting Hymns of Praise?
How loved and adored, old mama cats
That dawdle with pride o'er their kittens,
And mama cows that cherish their calves;
Birds hustling about to feed their young
While a star-eyed child, most loved of all!
Watches in a way as sacred as prayer.
A parade of bright flags, bands, and horses,
Great old reminder—This native land
Of brawny gods and mothers carving dreams
Of a land made safe and good for their young,
A Nation strong, with a heart for peace.
"Just give us time and peace we'll find!"
The end of the list of private loves
Is as far as the farthest recall.
'Tis good to remember, remember;
Like a silver chalice re-polished.
Loves come to us, O long forgotten
Till removed, the dull tarnish of plod.

MY FRIENDS ARE A SONG

Friends are a glowing fire that warms and warms
When you're sad, when you're cold and alone:
A peace that settles in with gentle warmth
Till brings the tingling joy that life is good.
O friends are the faultless part of yourself,
All the favorite things you'd like to be.
Our friends are God's very special gift,
Our cup that is always running over.

FROM WHENCE COMES LOVE?

*I could pick her up and she loved it,
Clucked and tittered with happy content.
If you've never stroked a silken hen,
You have a joy yet left in your box.
The wheelbarrow highly stacked with hay
For the waiting horses in the corral,
Susie flew on top and wouldn't budge.
Aye, hard it was to wheel the hayload.
To keep her in balance was my feat.
If we hit a bump and off she fell,
She'd fly right back and giggle, giggle.
When I dumped the hay, she'd screech and run.
But back she'd jump in the empty barrow
To ride where the hay was stored.
E'en today, I wonder why Susie
Loved and never feared her human friend.
No other found so naturally trusting...
All so apart from man's reckoning labs.*

MR. PRESIDENT

*O divine provision to lead mankind!
What God that gives His creation a man
Above the strength of even the strongest
And walks along to insure the journey.
O brave man who dares to such burdens,
Our respect, support, and grateful caring
Are all you ask of the people you serve.
Yet, little as it sounds to be, 'tis more
Than your countrymen oft' find to offer.
We slander, rebel, and vote to evict.
Though we know you've carried your load o'er
Trails unmarked to high and lasting summits.*

WHILE GARDENS GROW THEIR ROSES

All the world is filled with grace.
The prairie grows its Indian blankets,
The woodlands have their sweet bluets,
Deserts sculpture cacti giants!
While gardens grow their roses
'Mid the shasta daisy clumps,
Pink petunias line the walks
And ivy circles the elms.
But all of nature's glories
Don't compare with the blossoms
Of this one who carries to friends
Her blossoms of tender concern.

TILL TIME GIVES OUT

If several cows with calves are around,
One mother stays to watch the calflings
While others feed. Come danger, she bawls!
Like wind, cows rush, circle and butt.
Lions, tigers, bears, protect their young
Till they're old enough to fend for themselves.
But poor man with his well-birthed children
Nurtures frets with doubt till time gives out!

CHAPTER 17

HOW TO MAKE EARTH HEAVEN
(Published by Marshall Jones Company, 1992)

Making earth Heaven is something any of us would do if we could.

What if no eyes had been created to see the sky, the trees, flowers, horses, kittens, puppies, a baby's smile, a parent's love? No ears to hear the unending song of the mockingbird, the church organ, laughter?

What if man had been created without arms to hold a child? What if like fish we had no legs on which to walk among the glories of the earth?

What if we had to tell our food where to go and how to get digested? What if man had never been given teeth and had to drink his food? What if we had no nose to smell and enjoy the fresh morning air?

What if there was no means of thinking? What if we were as unthinking as, say, cow hide?

How do brain cells produce thinking? What material such as brains (which from animals we sometimes fry) can produce thinking?

When we realize how rich we are in our wonderfully self-run body we find ourselves in a Heaven of wealth, peace, and joy, even if we haven't a penny.

You say, try going without food, home, friends, and see how rich you feel!

Our greatest wealth is the Creator Himself Who is as permanent as $10 \times 10 = 100$. Don't think we can't get help from that direction! It may take Faith. But that is another part of our riches, faith some eaten food will get digested and replace cells!

Gratitude is another gift. Gratitude is as big a balance as faith.

"Huh! Hungry, jobless. Try then to think of something to be grateful for!"

We are such a small, unlearned part of the divine Creator's vast, infinite creation that to think of going it alone the way you are, is taking the highway to the City of Despair instead of the road to peace. The divinely-bestowed gift of feeling grateful just does something to us. We find an inner assurance that the Creator of the whole universe is, after all, the Creator of little old us! He made us to be a part of eternity along with the mountains and stars.

"Lotta good all that guff does me! All I want is something to eat!"

"Ask and it shall be given unto you."

"I have asked! Am asking! If you're so smart, give me a dollar."

"Here. Strictly from God Who sent me this direction."

When Christ said and proved (healing thousands) that Heaven is at hand, who has the gall to call him a liar?

"Except ye. . . become as little children ye shall not enter into the kingdom of heaven." (*Matt 18:3*)

We think of Heaven as a place where we are no longer conscious of age. Who thinks of Christ as old? Heaven will be an elating place for that reason alone; not old not young; just right.

He said, "God is a Spirit and they that worship Him must worship Him in Spirit and in truth. (*John 4:21*)

Christ Jesus was actually *sent to teach and to prove* to us how to be in the likeness of God, Spirit, thus automatically spiritual. It was the truth he promised would free us and it did each time he healed the sick or raised the dead because he knew the eternal spiritual you *is the only you.*

Remember it takes *faith.* Time and again Christ said, "Thy faith hath made thee whole."

We have a job to do to be free, and that is to *keep one with Spirit spiritual.*

"Hell, it's not worth it. Who has time to be that much of a saint? I'll take the crud of mortality. Big checks, big deals, pretty gals, steaks, ice cream, that good old money with enough left over to stash away for rainy days. What more could you ask?"

Where do you think all those satisfying things come from?

Christ said, "I can of myself do nothing."

He healed knowing it's God that wipes out mortal distress.

"What about when everything goes to hell? Bad sickness, tornados, earthquakes, late hard freezes that kill Spring's new start? I can't see any sense at all to what you're saying."

God the only good, there can be no evil in Good any more than 3+3=7.

"Then He isn't present in storms, war, hate?"

There is no way Good can be absent any more than truth can.

"Then He is in the tornado!"

Everything unkind is mortal. To God, Spirit, all is *spiritual.* If your home and family have been destroyed by a tornado and you lie helpless under the rubble, you are still Love's ideal as eternal as Love itself. This is the *real* and all else is the mortal lie of our being material mortals on our own. God Spirit is the truth that frees us. The spiritual you is the forever you!

"Does the hell raiser go to hell when he dies?"

As a parent you would expect him to straighten up. He's your own dear child. When you hurt others you get hurt, one of the best lessons the divine all Love has in Life's school. The murderer in his old age longs to be as murder-free as the rest of his family.

Our Father Mother God forgives our debts as we forgive our debtors or Christ Jesus would not have included this in our Lord's Prayer.

"You seem to have all life's questions answered. How have you reached such plausible conclusions?"

Our Christ has many ways of rescuing us. And this Christ who promised to be with us always is not someone who doesn't mean what he says.

However hard mortals try to leave God out, they can not succeed forever. Leaving God, Spirit, out is the difference between a beautiful, contented life and a life that has an emptiness nothing can fill.

We're all made by the Christ pattern who is our one example of man in the "likeness of God," as the Bible's first chapter declares.

God Spirit, man His likeness Spiritual, is what is meant by the Kingdom of Heaven being at hand.

Your job, keep spiritual.

CHAPTER 18

A BOWL OF REMEMBERING
(*Published by The Golden Quill Press, 1980*)

SELF PORTRAIT

I'm a part of treeless prairie
With its sage, its wine cups and yucca;
Part of the windmill's eternal song
Of buoyant hope and thirsts never quenched.

I'm a part of the ceaseless river,
The little boats that hunt for the sea,
Part of the ever-changing ocean
Where the drama of motion is played.

A part of the meadow's gentle life:
A wounded bird that sits in my hand
And asks to be loved and free again
And gets its wish after careful caring.

I'm a part of the loves of man, his
Dreams and nurtured seeds of timeless worth.
The earth is my home, my restful chair.
I am joy mixed with sorrow and peace.

THE CALM OF NOW

Now O now. Whatever now demands
The tools of yesterday fail to work;
Tomorrow's windlass is out of reach.
The calm of now brings its own release.

A BASKET OF SKY THINGS

Last week the sky had farm chores to do,
So donned its unbleached muslin apron
And swept with its wind bristled broom
Till every blade of grass and flower
Was dusty and tousled and cross.
Then by night here came a chariot
Brighter than you ever saw
Filled with its little promises of rain
That grew and spread and washed the earth clean.

TUTORS OF THE VALLEY

'Tis an holy thing, yon shelt'ring tree,
A massive pillar of strength and grace
With twisted trunk and far reaching limbs,
Craggy burls and bores where tree-tribes live,
The topmost branch a music hall for birds.
In the fall the leaves bear captured sunsets.

Ah, the greatness of one massive tree
Is ever-added strength upon strength
And a calm that asks for guileless trust
Through violent storms of adversity
Only hills and trees and saints e'er quell.
Still, thank I for such drills in holy heights.

LIFE'S WORST AGE

I can no longer be dirty
With garden mud on my clothes
And arbor leaves in my hair,
For on this horrible day,
O this horrible fifth of May,
I am a woman of thirty.

CLOWNS OF THE PRAIRIE

There's a fascinating combination
Of animal and vegetation
On the wide and never-ending prairie.

They call it a thistle but in the fall
It dries and forms a great mammoth ball,
A gray, prickly yet wooly thing that rolls.

Now, there comes a day when it longs to roam,
A gust of wind and this tumbling gnome
Rolls over and over in sheer delight.

Sometimes it reaches a fence and has to stop.
Then comes a whirl of wind that makes it hop
And again it goes on its windward way.

What a joke of nature these tumbling weeds
That tumble in herds to scatter seeds.
Who but the Maker would think of the like?

SWEET GLANCES

My oleander
Sways and swings
Its little pink hats
As if somewhere
In all the frills
Tiny children hide
And need to be rocked.

O FRIEND

When I die,
Take time to go to the prairie
And gather the flowers there.
It's where heaven's planted its best,
So rare in color and grace
You feel when you follow the draw
You've reached that Land of After While.

O when I die,
Don't send roses, glads, carnations.
Take time to go to the prairie
And gather any flower you see.
You'll love your stroll around heaven,
And who knows but there you'll find me?

CHAPTER 19

THE LAST KINK OF CIVILIZATION
(From The Sun Says When, Published By The Golden Quill Press, 1994)

War.

It's shocking to realize of all life on earth from grasshoppers, elephants, fish, to humans who consider themselves superior, none war thousands against thousands but man!

War is unheard of among animals. In fact, I have a cat and dog that adore each other.

Here is something to think about. We can't claim to be civilized until we remove the war kink!

My cat and dog get along perfectly because they were both acquired when but a few weeks old and didn't even think of themselves as different from one another.

The cat named Dickie Boy is a beautiful all black but for a bit of white at the throat and lower abdomen. Lying on his back I often say, "Your shirttail's out!" Prim, sleek, he walks like the king of the pack, caring not about his shirttail out!

Bored, he plays with his tail. When it moves slightly he tries to catch it. "Wham! I gotcha!" While the dog nearby takes a nap.

Danny Boy, a tan Chow pup is delighted with his playmate. They scamper and paw, unconscious of what we assume to be natural enemies.

Because of roaming coyotes, the cat isn't allowed to go outside till the coyotes tire of their roaming, around mid-day. The yard fenced, Danny Boy dog can go outside whenever he wishes. Once the cat shot out when the door was opened, dog and I after him. But the cat ran up a tree leaving us helpless.

I came in and prayed that He save this unusually loving beast. Never can I sit down, but here he is on my lap. So in the cat finally came, missing his man and dog he adores!

All of this proves that enemies *can* be friends, no devastating wars possible among friends!

We desperately need to take lessons from all God's creatures. Nothing at war but man we call superior to beast.

The whole of the universe is God expressing Himself in His creation, man especially, *made in His likeness.*

If cats and dogs can get along, why can't we work out some world-wide youth program where little ones (like kittens and pups) can grow up together, a huge nursery where children can learn and play together?

I can't think, sent home, they would want to grab a gun and shoot that kid across the aisle.

France, Italy, Germany, Russia. Kids love kids like pups love kittens.

Isn't it rather humiliating that children can get along, but grownups can't?

You say grown, hates take over.

Ah, not with my pets. The mighty rule of Love has never stopped.

It's another reason for us grownups to keep childlike, as the Bible says. "Except as ye become as little children..."

It's one of life's kinks man must face.

War eminent? Stop!

Are we or are we not superior to beasts?

GOOD PAYS GOOD

Winifred Mondell had been appointed Warden to fill the place of her husband who had died two years before. Two hundred prisoners were placed in her charge.

"They tell me you robbed a bank, son," she read on his chart.

"Yes," the young man answered quietly.

"How did you happen to do such a thing? Were you broke?" she asked in a friend-to-friend way.

"Owed money to my brother-in-law. There was another fellow who's had a lot of robbing experience and was sure we could pull off the deal."

"It's too bad you young men put so much trust in these older, experienced men. How much money did you get?"

"Four hundred sixty bucks."

"What then?"

"We headed for California - in a stolen car."

"Why did you finally confess?"

"They kept hounding me till I couldn't stand it."

"Your confession helps toward the sentence. Is this your first offense?"

He nodded.

"And last?"

He nodded.

"Good. Don't forget, you've made yourself a promise. This gives you stability. Do you have parents? This space is blank."

"My dad beat me for gettin' in with the wrong gang and my mom hated my doin's. Said I embarrassed her."

"Toby, remember your promise to yourself. Prison is no place for a boy like you. Take this place as a sort of home where you can get acquainted with your real self, somebody people look up to, with a loving wife and children. I see you're nineteen."

Toby felt drawn to this woman; someone he could really like."

"I want us to be real friends," she said.

"Thank you," he said shyly, looking down. "I'll try to be decent."

He was taken to his cell.

The shrieking bell announced the noon meal and brought guards who marched the prisoners to the dining room.

Toby marveled at the food: pork, slaw, beans and peach cobbler.

After the meal a red-head stepped up. "I'm Larz Green. We bunk together."

He didn't look like a guy that did real mean dirt stuff.

Suddenly Mrs. Mondell came up and said, "Boys, this is Toby Lawrence." Let's help him get acquainted.

Later he was taken to the fields where the prisoners worked. Assigned a special place, an old grizzly man came up and said, "This is where I work."

"I was assigned here," stated Toby.

"Think so? If you don't git, I'll start hoeing on you!"

Toby was getting mad enough to fight when suddenly the guard stepped up and pointed his gun at them.

"Either one of you'll make good targets if you don't shut up and get back to work."

One day Toby asked to see the Warden.

"Oh, Toby," she said. "No trouble, I hope."

"No. Worried about you."

"Me?" she smiled.

"I ain't no tattler, but…mean old man Pot Jones don't think when he's mad. He's too quick. I'd had my brains battered if the guard hadn't stepped up."

"Toby, I've been warned before. But a hand raised and the prisoner is shot."

He was relieved. Potts was a killer.

When Sunday came, they filed as usual into the chapel for morning service, followed by dinner and then off to the baseball field. Wow!

A year later, Toby was called to the Warden's office.

"Toby, I have good news for you."

"What?" he asked.

"I have received a parole for you from the governor. I sent in the recommendation because you have been one of the best behaved prisoners we have ever had and I want you to be free to go back and find a job. Remember: when you forget, the world forgets. But don't forget that officers will be watching you, ready to bring you back very quickly. But I have faith in you, Toby."

"I won't be back." There were tears in his eyes. Suddenly he put his arms around her. "I'll keep straight just for you. I promise." He'd found somebody he honestly liked.

Outside, the world wasn't forgetting. No job. Nothing.

His mom said, "My God, a release!"

"I behaved. I'm sorry and I'm going straight."

"Huh! We'll see," said his father.

Finally in the newspaper he found an ad offering a job digging potatoes. He went straight to it, a way to prove he was a hard, dependable worker.

One day the farmer's daughter came running. "Here's a letter for you. Are you a prisoner that's escaped? It says from the state penitentiary."

Those nearby stopped. Was he? His world tumbled. After all he *was* an ex-con.

The letter said: "Since you work has been farming, would it be possible for you to come as an officer to oversee the prison farming? I'm in need of a good, reliable person."

Toby couldn't stop laughing. Who says trying to go straight doesn't pay?

"Mom. Dad."

THE JOY OF DEATH

For most people death is feared and dreaded. It presents the unknown.

Will it come with an accident, or an illness? Will death itself hurt?

Will consciousness be forever silenced or will one wake up in some heaven or hell determined by how good or bad one has been? Maybe you can't believe in God enough to see Him as any help at such a time. Why, if so, wasn't he a help when your need was life-threatening?

Christ said God is the only Good. No evil can thus be attributed to God, all Good.

So how can ills have any other source but in man himself, his fears and doubts and unacceptance of God as a source of help?

"Why would God let His eternal ideas die?"

He doesn't. Ever. Christ proved this completely by raising the dead.

"But we still do die. Thousands a day, world over. Even children, tiny babies."

Ah, but you forget. What God all Good, all Spirit, sees is the spiritual you in His Spirit's likeness which is as eternal as He Himself. Our problem is we leave God out by thinking we are gods on our own.

It is very important to keep one's consciousness spiritual, in the likeness of spirit, God.

"Who can think dying is nothing to fear!"

Because we can know God all Love says, "Come, my child," through a beautiful door opening into a palace with fountains and flowers.

"How do you know so much? Have you been there?"

No. But Christ has. And He said Heaven is at hand.

"This old place?"

No. He meant it can be when you see God Spirit, thus His creation spiritual, as beautiful as we can imagine Heaven to be!

When we're spiritual we, the likeness of spirit, do see what God Spirit, sees. All so divine, so perfect. And with this the real Heaven not only is at hand when we die and shed our mortal coat, but we rise, ascend, as did Christ when he left his worshippers at the tomb.

Life is very complex to the mortal who is trying to be a good and useful citizen. And even though he may agree there is a better eternal life promised, he still may dread death so often preceded by disaster.

Maybe he's not ready to go. Maybe he sees no concrete proof that there's a Heaven to go to. If he hasn't been good enough he may end up in some purgatory or hell!

"You're right. I'll never think of dying as pleasant. Do you? Honestly?"

Yes. I'm expecting to see Christ, as well as others who have gone before me. As well as God Himself. Christ's love of our Father makes us know God is an infinite divine Parent who is all the Love expressed, claimed never absent, ever.

When you feel loved by family, friends pets, this is God Love expressing Love.

So how can we not take joy in such a reunion Those tiny children, that load of teens killed in a car wreck. Love cares. That eternal spiritual self is in the care of man's divine compassionate Father. Our future we do not know. We just know God is Love never absent and Love is as caring as the Christ who represented Him.

Any time He says come, I'm off.

Who can dread death when we continually get better till we're perfect? And make in God's likeness, we can well believe it will take forever!